Also by

Marisa P. Moris

and

Joseph P. Moris

Answers – Heaven Speaks

&

The Bible Speaks

Conversations with Jesus and the New Testament Authors

Book I Matthew and Mark

Book II Peter and John

Book III Luke and Paul

Book IV Jude and James

Marisa P. Moris and Joseph P. Moris

The Bible Speaks

Conversations with Jesus and the New Testament Authors

Book IV

Featuring

Jude and James

By

Joseph Moris

Marisa Moris

This book is dedicated to

Jesus Yeshua Christ

and all those "up there" who believe in this journey

Marisa P. Moris and Joseph P. Moris

The Bible Speaks

Copyright © 2015
by
Joseph P. Moris and Marisa P. Moris
Published by Intuition Publishing
Printed in the United States of America
ISBN 978-0-9898851-0-2
Intuition Publishing
1054 2nd Street
Encinitas, CA 92024
info@discoverintuition.com

Format and Cover by Marisa Moris
Edited by Joseph Moris
Cover Photo by Joseph Moris off the Carlsbad Calif. Coast
All rights reserved.
The contents of this book may not be reproduced in any form, except for short extracts for quotation or review, without the written permission of the publisher.
© Joseph P Moris and Marisa P Moris
First Published by Intuition Publishing
ISBN-10: 0989885151
ISBN-13: 978-0989885157
Transcriptions by Monica Harris and Lorna Muhlbach
Printed in the United States of America
First Edition: October 2016

Library of Congress Cataloging-in-Publication Data
The Bible Speaks
Joseph P Moris and Marisa P Moris
p.   cm.
1.) Religion 2.) Spirituality 3.) Christianity

Ephesians 4:2-5   King James Version
Author: Paul

With all lowliness and meekness, with longsuffering, forbearing one another in love; endeavoring to keep the unity of the Spirit in the bond of peace.

There is one body, and one Spirit, even as you are called in one hope of your calling:

One Lord, One Faith, One Baptism, One God and Father of all, who is above all and through all and in you all.

Ephesians 4:2-5   As paraphrased in Heaven Speaks

by: Joseph Moris

Always be humble and gentle. Because of your love, be patient with each other, making allowance for each other's faults.

Make every effort to keep yourselves united in the Spirit, binding you together with peace.

There is one body and one Spirit, just as also, you have been called to one glorious hope for the future.

CONTENTS

Introduction 1
Jude 8
Jude and Jesus 47
New Parable from Jesus 99
Prologue to Jude 101
Author's Note Regarding Muhammed 116
James 124
James Clarification 164
James Review about Christ, Joseph and James 169
Judas 219
Conclusion to the Bible Speaks books I-IV 239
Epilogue 241
Jesus Speaks 241
Jesus's Wrap-up and Last Comments on The Bible Speaks series 245
Authors Page 250

Introduction

This is now the fourth and last of The Bible Speaks Author's books. There will be a fifth book in this series but it will be entitled "*Ask Jesus*". This fifth book will be a collection of thoughts by Jesus as well as a compilation of some of the "lost" parables that never found their way into the New Testament.

Rather than repeat the introductions found in the first three books in The Bible Speaks series a brief recap is all that should be necessary.

Marisa has a seizure disorder and while driving in 2009 she had a seizure. While convulsing and then succumbing to the seizure by becoming unconscious while driving, her car crossed the median into oncoming traffic. Oncoming traffic avoided her but her car came to rest when she hit a fire hydrant. Marisa's sunroof was open and very quickly her car filled with water before help could arrive. She was attended to by passersby and then when the paramedics arrived she was quickly revived. But in that brief period of passing over to the "other side" Marisa had an out-of-body spiritual experience and she met an angel.

Standing next to the angel and looking down on her lifeless human body in the car, Marisa categorically stated "I don't want to be her anymore....I don't want to go back". The angel said "you have much to do and it is not yet your time". The next thing Marisa remembered was being at the hospital. She remembered the angel and began wishing she could see and speak to that angel again. She wanted to know why it was so important for her to come back to a hard life when she could have just stayed over in heaven where there was so much peace.

Marisa has never been religious much less spiritual. She only went to church as a child because we, her parents forced her to go. Once she was an adult and out on her own, religiosity and spirituality was the furthest thing from her mind. But after this experience she had a burning desire to learn more about the "other side". For over a year she consulted with and read up on others who had also visited the "other side" due to near death experiences. In her quest she became infatuated with the construction of heaven and specifically the "trinity". She studied up on God, the Holy Spirit and Christ. By 2011 Marisa had a better understanding of Christ and his journey to earth as a human in the form of Yeshua ben Joseph, or as we better know him, as Jesus.

On Easter morning of 2011 while taking a bath Marisa baptized herself in the name of Christ and she cried like a baby. We have since come to understand that when we do good and we tear up from doing or seeing good then that is the evidence of the aroused or ignited Holy Spirit within us. Nevertheless, shortly after her baptism strange things started to happen. In *Heaven Speaks*, our first book, both Marisa and I explain where we are today and how we got to the point we are at now with trying to bring powerful words from Christ, Jesus and the Authors of the New Testament to a 21st century world; how a Christian father dealt with the abilities of a special daughter who could now see "the other side" and communicate with it and how Marisa was going to put her special abilities to work for good…for the light…and to not just be a "psychic or fortune teller". Marisa has been instructed that her purpose is to bring light from heaven…. not to prophesy and tell people who their next boy or girl friend is or how to win the lottery.

In *Heaven Speaks* I tell the story about the death of one of my bible study classmates in 2011. I convinced Marisa to join me at church service not long after Easter when Marisa, not knowing my classmate's wife, whispered in my ear and while pointing asked who a certain lady was. I told her I would tell her later. Later didn't happen as we got busy after the church service and quickly went our separate ways. About a week later Marisa called me to tell me that an "apparition" had appeared to her. The apparition called himself Bill. She said he was a young handsome man who was leaning up against the wall with one hand in his pocket who told Marisa that he needed to let his wife know that he was perfectly fine in heaven and that she needs to live her life to the fullest but when her time comes he will be right there at the door as she crosses over to heaven.

Marisa asked me if I knew what and who she was talking about. She didn't know this 'Bill' or his wife. I then told her that my friend from my bible class had passed away and that when we had been in church the week before and she had pointed to someone in the pews that it just so happened to be Bill's wife. Marisa then told me that she had asked me who she was because during the service she was seeing all these sparkles dancing around Bill's wife. She said that it must have been "Bill" that she was seeing. I scoffed at first but then I had to decide whether it was prudent to let Bill's wife know that we were given a message for her.

That following Sunday I went to church alone without Marisa and there, sitting among others was Bill's wife. By now several weeks had passed since Bill's passing but his wife still looked quite forlorn with sad eyes and drooping shoulders. When the service was over I sat in my chair trying to decide what best to do for as a Christian, I was well aware that there are numerous passages in the Old and New Testament that prohibit seeking out "psychics and seekers of the dead" so this was something that was grinding on my mind. Do I trust the Bible or do I trust my daughter???? That was the big question.

After the church service was over and as I continued sitting in my chair I noticed Bill's wife had stood and walked over to a huge strand of rose bushes. She was standing with several others while surrounded by rose bushes and I could only see everyone's heads and shoulders. I knew there was no way I was going to jump into the middle and interrupt the group so I closed my eyes and said "okay God.... this is your ballgame...if you want me to talk to Bill's wife then either give me a sign or I'm outta here". My initial instincts (or better yet...fear) were to let it all go but when I opened my eyes Bill's wife was standing all alone in the bushes. There was no sight of all the others who had just been speaking with her. I looked around and none of them were in sight. I couldn't believe it. I wondered, where did they all go so fast as all this occurred in the course of literally seconds while I was talking to God. Seeing that she was now alone some force got me out of the chair and before I could realize it I was standing in front of Bill's wife. She gave me a sad smile and said hello. I told her that Bill was a member of my bible class and that I felt really bad for her that she had lost her soulmate.

Because of the courtesy of making introductions just prior to church starting I had met her a couple times before but only briefly. She did not know anything about me nor me of her. Nevertheless, I looked her in the eye and with a quivering voice and all the courage I could muster I told her that I had a message for her. I told her that Bill had appeared to my daughter and that Bill had a message for her. I told her what Bill had told Marisa. With that she just broke down crying. Needless to say I was freaked out. I knew how my pastor and his wife felt about anyone who would have Marisa's ability so here I was, in close proximity to my pastor and I have Bill's wife weeping in front of me when all of a sudden she begins to laugh within her sobs and she gives me a huge hug.

Bill's wife said that Bill had had over 20 stints put into his heart during his lifetime and that every single time he was on the gurney and on his way into the operating room he would squeeze her hand and tell his wife that if he died during the operation he would find a way to come back and let her know he was okay in heaven. Despite being very faithful followers of Jesus, she never really believed him but now she was being told by a perfect stranger that Bill was communicating from the other side.

I now see Bill's wife from time to time at the gym and she looks happy again and full of life. My pastor and his wife were not so happy about what happened and basically showed me the door. They were freaked by it all and thought it was evil. In fact, every strong Christian that I meet tells me that what we are doing is wrong and that we are being led by the devil. It's quite frustrating but I understand why they feel that way.

From that first occurrence Marisa's abilities swung dramatically from seeing "dead" people to seeing and conversing with the angels and more specifically Christ, Jesus and the Holy Spirit. She has since learned that the "angel" she met on the other side was actually Marisa's higher self.... her "big" Marisa.... the offspring of her soul that created the spirit that lives now within Marisa.

Over the last five years Marisa has become really good buddies with Jesus as her abilities have increased exponentially. Marisa sees and hears from the universe in general now and with Jesus she speaks with him daily. He has given Marisa the ability to see other creations of Christ including Master Guides and other "beings" that encircle the earth taking care of us humans. For we have learned that we are all spirits stuck in human bodies and that our spirits know heaven but our human minds do not. We dubbed that dichotomy in *Heaven Speaks* as we humans having amnesia.

We are told that we are human animals with mind and ego and we are filled with a spirit that knows the path we are supposed to take in this life but our human minds just don't listen. In our second book in this bible speaks series featuring John and Peter we are told by Peter and again in another example by Jesus, that the "other side" speaks for example, at 20 mhz but that our minds are zooming along at 100 mhz. We humans just don't know how to quiet our minds so that we can listen, learn and react to what Christ, through his "clones" that live in each of us has in mind for us on this earth.

Because of her abilities and the completion of our first book *Heaven Speaks*, Marisa and I decided to have more taped sessions and pursue something that twists my mind and that is the evidence of numerous mysteries found around the earth. I am so curious to find out why there are pyramids all over the earth yet no one can truly explain how and why they exist; why there are cities under water around the globe and why crop circles and non-indigenous structures in places like Easter Island exist. Therefore, for our second book we decided to try to find out the answers to some of these earthly mysteries in deference to spiritual and universal mysteries.

In 2014 we turned on the tape recorder and started asking questions about the earth's mysteries. We learned a lot but strictly as an "aside" and at the end of that first session I asked if Jesus could come into our channeled session and he did. I then asked him a question off the subject. I asked him something about Paul, the Roman who at one time killed Christians for sport but then became the author of thirteen books in the New Testament. Jesus appeared and said "ask him yourself" when Paul appeared to Marisa.

After asking Paul a question to which he responded I turned to Marisa and said I'd rather interview the authors of the New Testament than to write a book just yet on earth's mysteries and that is when we pivoted to these books instead. The first three books included Matthew and Mark, then Peter and John, then Paul and Luke and now this, the fourth book is our interviews with Jesus's brothers who are also authors of the New Testament, Jude and James.

Hopefully you have been able to read the first three editions in this series of *The Bible Speaks* but don't worry if you haven't. It is not necessary to read them in order. James and Jude are quite extraordinary individuals and we think you will enjoy their stories. It has never been our intent to open a bible and ask these authors why they said what they said in their scriptures. These books are meant to give the reader a better understanding of who these authors were instead of what we already know by their writings. So, hopefully you will be intrigued by coming to learn who these men (and the women who are also followers of Christ) are and how their advice and words can bring more meaning to your lives.

Jesus told us that anyone who reads the words in these books will have his spirit with them at that very same time. Yes, as you read these pages you will have Jesus sitting right there with you even though you don't see him or hear him but believe me, he's there.

With no further ado, here are Jude and James, Jesus' brothers.

Jude

Jude was nothing like what I expected. I guess this is becoming a consistent theme. That may be why Jesus wants us to do this book so that all those willing to read these words will then be able to put into context the Authors and Apostles as they really were in the time of Jesus rather than just faces on a DaVinci painting.

We had had some brief encounters with both Jude and James in previous recordings but not substantial enough to start their books so you may see some references to both James and Jude where you might scratch your head and ask "well, what did they say then?". We have done our best to incorporate previous meetings into these texts nonetheless.

Here's Jude….and…remember, his book is the last book of the New Testament before Revelation and it is only one page long so hopefully this gives you a better idea of who Jude was.

(Whenever you find the text in bold print that is added text that came from re-reading the original manuscript. Marisa and I never like to leave anything to chance so we always re-read our manuscript for

corrections, errors or additions that "they" may want to include, take out or correct. We start right out with additions that come two years after commencing our first conversations)

Marisa: Okay. Today is June 14th 2016 and we're going to re-read our rough manuscript from what we initially received back in July 2014 when we started on the James and Jude interviews. It's 11:24, and we're going to say a prayer. Heavenly Father, God, we come together today to do this review of Jesus' brothers, James and Jude. We ask that you guys please come forward. We ask that Jesus, you surround this room, surround the house with the Light of Christ protecting us, guiding us and leading us. We ask if there are any Archangels; Archangel Michael, Gabriel, Uriel, Raphael if they can surround this room, surround the house, and protect us from any tricksters or any false energies. And we ask that – Poochie's taking in Jesus.

Joe: She's under the couch digging? She only does that where Jesus is standing.

Marisa: Yeah...as if I've never seen her do something like that before. It's so funny. Okay, and then we just ask our guides, angels and teachers to be here to assist, and I think I want to have a gatekeeper today. Who's a good gatekeeper? I'm hearing Paul say that he can do it. Okay. Paul, you're gatekeeper then, or whoever is for our highest and best – oh, there's Samuel. Okay. And then let's see if you guys can do this without zapping Papa's energy. They laughed. Okay. Amen. We're good. All right, here we go. I'm ready. I'm already all warm, because all the guides are in my energy but James wants to talk. Do we want to hear from everyone in here or do we just want to review Jude? Everyone is always anxious to talk.

Joe: I know, but we're doing Jude first. We're not doing James *first. Jude is first. Is Jude in here, or shall I jump all the way down to James?*

Marisa: They say, "We have appeared. We came upon, we came upon the midnight sky, and as we dropped upon this earth, we said unto you, we will live here, and that's –" .... I'm seeing what's-his-name walking in now. It's Jude.

Jude Interview 7-15-14

Marisa: Let's start recording. Okay, today is -- it's 10:00, July 15th*, Tuesday. It's 10:03 actually*

Joe: You've already said a prayer.

Marisa: Yeah. I've already said the prayer.

Joe: You protected everything? It's just not on the tape, that's all.

Marisa: Yeah, exactly. So Jude --.

Joe: In our last session we were asking for James and Jude and they said Tuesday. So it's Tuesday.

Marisa: Okay.

Joe: So I wonder if Jesus is here --.

Marisa: It's James --.

Joe: -- and if he can bring his brothers James and Jude in.

Marisa: Those are his brothers?

Joe: Yeah.

Marisa: So, Jude is kind of --. Sorry, Jude but you're kind of creepy looking.

Joe: He was creepy last time.

Marisa: He was?

Joe: Said that a little bit last time.

Marisa: He has that cue-ball head and he's kind of creepy looking. He's got no hair, and he reminds me of the creepy eunuch on Game of Thrones. He has the robe on and his hands in the pockets, you know. Kind of has like, sorry Jude, but it's kind of like – I don't know if it's like pervy energy.

Joe: I don't know. We'll figure it out, but I was thinking about that the other day.

Marisa: Is that really him?

Joe: I mean you look at people and we're fortunate because we came out normal looking. But I see people and they have various deformities, and you just think, oh my gosh, you know. They're not attractive to people and what have you. But it's not their fault.

Marisa: Yeah.

Joe: So it doesn't really matter what Jude looks like. He was there, he grew up with his brother. I want to find out how long he was there. In other words, what was their gap in ages?

(Jude) 13 years.

Joe: Wow. Then he didn't – Jude couldn't possibly have known a whole lot about Jesus' life at home because Jesus had left. Didn't he say somewhere in our other interviews that he left home and started on his travels around the age of nineteen? If so Jude would have only been about six or seven years old when

Jesus left.

Marisa: Was Jude a warrior? I want to make sure that this is the right guy in here, because Jude just turned from the creepy bald guy with his hands in his pockets, like in-front-of-the-monk robe, and he's got these weird little beads around his neck almost. He says they're for inter-dimensional travel, and he's coming from a different dimension. But then when I pulled him forward into my field, he looks like he's wearing like a – like the type of outfit you see Archangel Michael wearing, like the skirt, the battle skirt, you know how like they have like a sword?

Joe: Yeah.

Marisa: That's what – that's what Jude looks like now.

Joe: Mmm. No, I don't think so.

Marisa: Who is this guy sitting – oh, is that Archangel Michael? Oh, I've never seen Archangel Michael before. I can actually see him – he looks like a man. He has the battle skirt on, and he's got a –

Joe: My understanding is James is the number two child.

Marisa: Oh no, he says they're seven years apart, but they were together for 13 years. Okay so Jude was seven years after Jesus and they were together for 13 years. Jude says Jesus got more attention than him.

Joe: Well, those are the kind of questions I want to ask him. Is Jude ready for me to ask questions? And then we'll talk to James?

Marisa: Jude, I'd like to ask if you could please step forward. We really appreciate you coming in tonight. He says:

(Jude)   *"I would like to share my words and thoughts."*

Joe: Please do.

(Jude)   *"For not many have listened to me."*

Marisa: Didn't he write a book?

Joe: He wrote a very short book in the Bible but, I mean, that's all that Constantine used.

Marisa: Okay, don't tell me too much. He says:

(Jude)   Not many want to listen to me, for I am just the under-shadow of that which was greatness. There was never a dull moment, at least not for him. I stood tall and I still look short. I stood mediocre for then that appeared as failure. This is the way that my mind worked while I was human and this emotion and feeling came through in my writing. There was never a dull moment. But as I wrote about the missionary that is known as my brother, the depictions that were made, the opinions that were written (by me) were removed and stricken once, twice, thrice times.

Marisa: What does that mean?

Joe: By Constantine when they were putting the Bible together? Did they edit his writings? Is that what he means? They edited it? Shortened it? Cut it out?

(Jude)   Yes, absolutely, they did edit it. The many things the conscience within me, or you would say the Holy Spirit within me, kept me from sharing the truth about things that may make certain people look bad. So I removed them or those who knew what I wrote removed them. But not everything! I tell the truth *and only the truth.*

Joe: *What is the truth?*

(Jude) *But those that do not have the ears to hear do not listen.*

Joe: *But we are here so we are here to listen. And Jude, you are for our highest and best good aren't you?*

Marisa: *Let's see. Jude, are you for our highest and best? I'm not going to ask him. I'm going to ask ...*

Joe: *Ask Jesus.*

Marisa: *Alpheus or Jesus, is Jude --? Is this version of Jude in here for our highest and best good?* **"Yes".** *Is he in 100% resonance with the Christ consciousness?* **"Yes".** *Is he --?*

Joe: *This is going to be very interesting. I really want to hear what he has to say. He feels like he's been in Jesus' shadow, even though he stood tall, and then the truth as he wanted to say it, was stricken. But if him being here is for our highest and best good I want to hear it even if it made others, somebody else, look bad.*

Marisa: *Abraham, is he for our highest and best good?* **"Yes".** *Yeshua? Eden, is he for our highest and best good?* **"Yes".**

Joe: *Let's hear it, Jude. Let's hear it. What is it? Get it off your chest. I want to hear what it is that's --. Jesus does not want us to go negative. He does not want us to put down anything that detracts from the faith..... we can't go negative on this. So --.*

(Jude) *There are many things that cannot be taken off my chest, for some things shall not be told. Some things shall not be told, indeed. But --.*

Joe: If you want to tell them, you can tell them.

(Jude)   --An understanding of that which is, and that which was, is something that may bring turmoil, but it also may bring hope and belief to many.

Joe: Wow. I want to hear it. I want to hear it all.

(Jude)   For, there are truths about many of the brethren, as they say, the brothers, the sisters of the missionary groups. There are --.

Joe: Is he talking about his immediate family, his immediate brothers and sisters? Or is he talking about the women who followed Jesus, or the men who followed Jesus?

Marisa: He's talking about the family --.

(Jude)   I speak of the family that became family, that was not blood, but may be stronger than blood. For, we gave our lives for the cause. We gave our lives indeed. For, there are many who had romances that were said to have never had romances. For the church is based on the priests not having romance due to the fact that it is said that you cannot have God and romance together. This is the belief that I see at this time. But for one to use my brother as an example of never having had romance is incorrect.

Joe: Which brother? Are you talking about Jesus or are you talking about James?

(Jude)   "Talking about Jesus."

Joe: Is he talking about his romance with Mary Magdalene?

(Jude)   "Oh, you already know."

Joe: We're guessing Jude. We're guessing, because we know that there was --- in the Bible itself we know that there was a special relationship there. But it's all been speculation.

(Jude)   Yes, special indeed. For, there was a girl prior to this. For we both had love for her. Sarasita. [It's not like Mexican. It's like Sarasita something.]

Marisa: They were 13.

Joe: What's that?

Marisa: That's what – I just heard him say – first of all, he's the third child, not the second. In the beginning – he keeps saying, "I'm the third. I'm the third. I'm the third. I'm the third," and I didn't want to interrupt, but he keeps saying it so…

Joe: That's not my understanding. I thought he was like last. Ahead of him was… oh, Mary had James, and then she had – well, maybe she did have Jude in there. Because I know she had a son by the name of Daniel, and a son by the name of Joseph, and I think it was either Daniel or Joseph that died.

Marisa: One of them died, and I think it was the first one, is what he's saying. He's saying the second, because what he was saying was the third, the second living one died, but he kept saying, but I didn't know if I was just making it up, but if you're saying now that one died then it was probably the first one. I think we're seeing in opposite. I could be seeing the 7 flipped upside down, so it could technically be the fourth, and the last one died instead of the first one?

Joe: Well, if they're seven years apart – they used to have kids every year back then. So – anyway, let's just keep going with what he's got.

Marisa: Well, he said the second kid in there is somewhere, so he just said to switch it to the third. So then that would mean that Jude is the third.

Joe: Well –

Marisa: Because we have in there the second, so that would mean that we're saying that Jude's the second one.

Joe: Yeah, because Mary had a couple of girls in there too, and then she had a – I think it was Miriam and another Mary, and then after their son Joseph was born or died, their father Joseph died. Was she with another man after Joseph died?

Marisa: There were babies from another man.

Joe: What's that?

Marisa: She had babies from other men, he said.

Joe: Who did?

Marisa: The mom.

Joe: Mary?

Marisa: Uh-huh. Two.

Joe: Mother Mary?

Marisa: Uh-huh.

Joe: Whoa. Nobody's going to believe that. I mean, nobody like that would – oh, my God, that would create a real maelstrom with the church.

Marisa: He's saying eleven total children. She had seven with one man, one died, two with someone else. When she was later in her years.

Marisa P. Moris and Joseph P. Moris

Joe: Wow.

Marisa: So maybe her husband died? She had a son named Michael or something.

Joe: My understanding is that Jesus was about 13 or 14 when Joseph died and he had to take over the family. And therefore he couldn't go to school like other Jewish boys at that age because he had to take care of the family. Normally the Jewish boys would go off to school at the age of 13 but Jesus couldn't do that. According to some books I've read, when his father died working on Herod's palace he had to take care of the family for Mary had all these little kids.

Marisa: Oh, okay.

Joe: And then when Jesus was about 19 or 20, then he could leave, but James who was the eldest underneath him took over the family and became the head of the family.

Marisa: It looks like there were two James. Not James the author. It feels like there were two brothers named James.

Joe: Well, John – John the – not John, the Baptist, but John who did the book of Revelation, his brother's name was James, and he also was a disciple or an apostle.

Marisa: It feels like there were two James that were related to Jude and Jesus and Mary didn't have them all.

Joe: Oh.

Marisa: It's like why did they name all their kids Mary and James when they all have the same name?

Joe: I don't know, I really don't.

Marisa: Anyways, okay. Well, yeah, Jude is the third kid and yeah, it does feel like there's two James. It feels like there's a really young one, which is probably from the other father, like the youngest one, and that's the one that's in here, I think. And then there's James that's like around the same age as Jesus.

Joe: Is Jesus here right now?

Marisa: Yeah, he's right here.

Joe: Let's ask him, because he's going to know who his family is.

Marisa: Yeah. He says – let's see here.

Joe: Where – did he have – well, let's ask Jesus. Did his mom end up getting married to another man after she lost – after Joseph died?

(Jesus) "Yes."

Joe: About how old was she when Joseph died?

Marisa: Twenty-seven, it seems. Twenty-seven.

Joe: How old was she when she had Jesus?

Marisa: Looks like 14.

Joe: Okay. So she was definitely with Joseph long enough to have a whole bunch more kids.

Marisa: And she had one before – let's see. One before Jesus. Let me see. Is Jesus the first? No. Jesus was her first.

Joe: She had one before?

Marisa: No, he was the first. And then there was another and then there was Jude, and then there was – looks like there was a Michael or something like that, or a David. One of them died. I can't tell if it's the first kid. No. It's the last kid died.

Joe: *I still can't imagine Jude being the third kid if there's seven years apart, because in those days, they just had a kid every year.*

Marisa: *Yeah, that's why I'm saying I think one died.*

Joe: *So she had Jesus, and then she had James, and then she had a child that died, and then she had Jude?*

Marisa: *I feel like she had – this is going to be totally against the Bible. Like she had one that died first, and then Jesus – hold on a second, No, no no. Jesus says,*

(Jesus) *"I was the first that she was pregnant with, and then there was a child that died. She believed that she was barren. She believed that she could not have children, and she was always told that she could not have children. This is why when she became pregnant, it was a miracle, because she was always told that she would not have children."*

Marisa: *So – let me see here.*

(Jesus) *"So she had unto, brought unto this world, that which is me. And then there was a child, a child that died. One year, two months passed, and this is when, this is when James, this is when James was conceived. James was then born and then two years later is when Jude was born."*

Joe: *Oh, okay.*

Marisa: *And then there was a Matthew or a David that was like crippled. Was it Matthew? David. David that was crippled, and then I think after that, it looks like a Jededius ... Jehious.... I can't really say the name, but he was real strong and a big bully. And I think that's when Joseph died. No, there was one more. And then Joseph died, and then three* *years later, she was too old to bear children. She was like 30. She had two kids, twins – nope, not twins, like Irish twins, one after the other.*

Joe: *Oh, okay.*

Marisa: *That's what he was – that's what he's showing me. There's one more kid in there that I missed. There's a couple girls. Is that true, Jesus? He says, "Yeah, that's true."*

Joe: *Oh, okay.*

Marisa: *He says you can – he says,*

(Jesus) *"You can look at this many different ways." He says, you can look at it as if my mother was a virgin." He says, "Or you can say that it was a miracle that she had a child because she was supposedly barren, and they said – prophets said unto her…"*

Marisa: *I think they were like in a mystical group where they would pray, and everybody would lay in the middle, you know, and they would like pray around them, might seem like people floating. I don't think that's – do they really float? He says,*

(Jesus) *"No. You're just seeing that in your mind. The religious groups in which she came from, she was told that she would not bear fruit."*

Joe: *Well, obviously they were wrong.*

Marisa: *Yeah. That's why he's saying it was a miracle to them, to the group that they were a part of, where they said she actually had a child, she actually had a child, because it looks like they put her in the middle of a circle and said, "If there is to be a Messiah, or if there is to be this, let this barren woman have this child," or something like that. It was like this long,* like a – look at – like almost like a ritual, and then within ten months she was pregnant. So he's showing all this – they at least show me – Mary Magdalene wears the same thing, like these red coats. They're like women in red coats. They're very powerful like mystical healer women. And it looks like Mary was a daughter of one of those or something. Looks like – what was her mom's name? Anna? Anne.

Joe: Don't know.

Marisa: Anne's an Ascended master.

Joe: Don't know. Bible didn't talk about Joseph and Mary's parents.

Marisa: Yeah, and Anna is the grandmother of Jesus. He says,

(Jesus) "This is my grandmother. My grandmother was and is an Ascended master, for she is from a different soul pod than we are from. She's not from ours but entered into the earth plane to bring about a revolution, a change, a strength to women, a monarchy-type energy to the planet, to the world."

Marisa: He's showing that she was very powerful.

Joe: Mary's mother?

Marisa: Uh-huh, Mary's mother. And, that she was very psychic, and she was a prophetess. She could see the future, and she saw that Mary could have no children. Is this all true, Jesus? Yeah, okay. I'm just making sure I'm channeling you. He says,

(Jesus) "Yes, yes." He says, "Many times you will block what I'm saying, and that is out of fear of your father getting scared or out of you getting scared that people are going to be upset. Just channel me, dear one. Just channel *me, dear one, and if you don't want to put it in the book, don't put it in the book."*

Marisa: He says, "You are so afraid. We're like, 'Dude, don't tell Marisa, oooh, oooh,' but that's kind of silly if we're trying to write a book of truth, and we're blocking them." He says, "I'm telling you, I'm telling you," And he says, "And this is me, look it's me." He's like showing me his energy. He doesn't have any darkness on him. He says,

(Jesus) "This is I," he says. He says, "Once you feel and know the truth within you, once you feel and know the truth within you, it will all make so much more sense, because you will see the Bible really is very accurate. They just saw it a different way. They just saw that a miracle, that a barren woman had a child and they saw this as a miracle. The church then turns this into a different type of miracle. So in essence, this will help you –"

Marisa: He's pointing at me.

(Jesus) "– to believe more because in your heart, you know that many things that are written in the Bible just do not feel right."

Marisa: Okay. Thank you. Now he's saying that I'll be able to believe more.

Joe: Oh, okay.

Marisa: That's interesting. Yeah, because sometimes you just read something, and you're like, "Really?" Yeah, that doesn't make sense.

Joe: Yeah.

Marisa: Anyways, okay.

(Jude) But the feelings that man has for a woman --.

Joe: Wait a minute. How old was Jesus then when he had a flirtatious feeling toward Sarasita.

(Jude): I was 12.

Joe: And he's seven years older, so he was 19.

(Jude): He was 19.

Joe: So Jesus was somewhat like a normal teenager. He had feelings --.

(Jude): Yes. There are many that say that he was godlike from birth, and I can say that he was not.

Joe: That's what I want to know.

(Jude): He was a regular person but received much attention because of the fact that he was born differently, or so we have been told.

Joe: By his mom? By Mary? Mother Mary? By his aunt Elizabeth?

(Jude): By the priestess by the fire.

Marisa: There! That's what I'm seeing. A priestess. I'm seeing – yeah. Oh, my God! Okay. That's exactly what I'm seeing.

Marisa: He's showing like, not a priest, but a priestess. Let *me see. Are you still for our highest and best good? He is. Okay, he's confusing me.]*

Joe: This is going to be something that I'm going to want to talk to Jesus about.... Jesus is going to have to clarify all of this. But I've always assumed that Jesus grew up as a regular kid.

Marisa: Let me talk to Jude's higher self. If I'm tapping into him in that lifetime, like they just said, because he's incarnated and we can't reach him, I'm feeling how nervous he is right now. My stomach. I want to throw up. So, are we getting an earthbound version of him? No?

Joe: They said this was for our highest and best good.

Marisa: Jesus says, "The reason why your stomach was sick at the time was because you could hear what we were saying, but you were afraid of your father's judgment, or you were afraid that he was going to say that you are channeling Satan."

Joe: Oh.

Marisa: So I was more scared of what you were going to think –as opposed to what they were saying. That's what he's saying. Like I didn't want you to go, "Oh, no. We're going to stop all the books. That's it. We're done. This is Satan." He says,

(Jesus) "Both of you have evolved and grown so much since this time (two years), and this is one of the reasons why we have the books broken up. This is one of the reasons why, because we knew that the review of these books, time would pass, maturity would come to your abilities and your ability to see. At that time, you did not have the ability to see. You had the ability to channel. You had the ability to ask questions and receive yes/no answers, and you had the ability to know

whether something was close or far and this is how you determined whether something was in your energy or not, but as you can see we are all in your energy, even Jude, even though he is hundreds of feet –"

Marisa: Like he's like way up there, like if I'm the middle of the clock, he's outside the clock, like five clocks away. He says,

(Jesus) *"This is also your energy. If you see it, we're in your energy. It just does not mean that we – we may just be as you have said in the past, 'skyping in,' so Jude is in another place, and he is using the device that's on his neck."*

Marisa: It's like a necklace.

(Jesus) *"Using the device that you see upon his neck which does not really look like that. You are just seeing it like that so that your mind can understand that he has something on him that is allowing him to broadcast his frequency into your field so that you may see him and talk to him, but it is as if he is here with us even though he is not physically here with us, for he isn't. He's in an incarnation somewhere else in time. He's incarnated, but his higher self is Adam."*

Joe: Really?

Marisa: Yeah, like yours.

Joe: What?

Marisa: Yeah.

Joe: Whoa.

Marisa: So his higher self – because when you said let's call in his higher self, Adam popped up.

Joe: Oh, okay.

Marisa: **Yeah. Interesting. Okay.**

Marisa: Am I out of my mind? Is it really --? I never felt nervous before when I looked --. Let me see. Samuel, can you come in?

Joe: He's the last book of the Bible before the Book of Revelation. Almost like an afterthought.

Marisa: Don't tell me too much. Don't tell me. I don't want to get any seeds planted.

Joe: No, I can understand why he's already used the metaphor for being tall but feeling so short. He was Jesus' brother but Jesus was getting all the attention.

Marisa: Oh, okay. So he's basically showing some peninsula island showing the – I think he's showing where he died.

Joe: I was just going to ask that. Where was he --? Was he persecuted and killed, or exiled?

Marisa: He's showing some sort of deserted island.

Joe: Why? Why was he there? They arrest him?

Marisa: They arrest you? "No". Was he running? "No". It looks like he died of old age.

Joe: Did he just become a recluse?.... Instead of a disciple?

Marisa: He says he spread the word but he spread the truth and people didn't believe him.

Joe: Tell me the truth. What is the truth? Don't be afraid Jude because I'm going to clarify with Jesus anyway.

Marisa: Jude says, "Thanks. Thanks, man."

Joe: He said, "Thanks"?

Marisa: Tell me the truth, because I'm going to clarify with Jesus anyways.

Joe: Oh.

Marisa: And he says, "Thanks, man."

Joe: Oh.

Marisa: Because like, you know, "Tell me the truth. I trust you, because I'm going to clarify with your brother anyways that overshadowed you." Hahahahaha. It was Peter imitating him. Peter goes, "Oh, thanks, man." Like, joking. That was funny. That wasn't Jude, though.

Joe: Sarcasm.

Marisa: Yeah, they were being sarcastic. It was Peter and Jude – Jude's actually closer now.

Joe: Sounds like Jude wanted to punch me or something.

Marisa: Jude actually just punched Peter, but like he says, "Hey, man, this is my thing." He's very possessive about getting his time.

Joe: Jude? Yeah, I got that.

Marisa: Yeah. He's very like, "Hey, man, get out of my spotlight," because Peter came in and was like, "Hey, thanks, man." [Sound of hand slapping] I don't think they really punched. It's just the energy, the way my mind is reading it. That's funny. Okay. What the guides are saying right now is that this book alone, what we're channeling today and reading could be a book that you just sat down and wrote, instead of having all the transcripts, like you could just listen to it and say, "We were told by Jesus, da da da, this and that," and then put a little thing in that says, you know, it was a miracle or that she was – they're saying you're not even going to put that in there. They don't want a bunch of stuff in here where you're going to get judged by your pastors and stuff like that, but at the same time, it's like – they said that this is part of the lost teachings of Jesus.

Joe: Oh.

Marisa: That's what it is. Okay. So they're bringing in information for the other – the lost teachings of Jesus is because if we're going to teach – we're going to bring in the lost parables of Jesus, we can also bring in the lost story of his miracle birth.

Joe: Mmm, okay. Well, let's see how this plays out. I'm just wanting to read through this initial manuscript and they can say whatever they want to say, and then I'll deal with the transcript when I'm putting the book together.

Marisa: Exactly.

(Jude): The truth is that my brother was my brother. He was human. He was no god. There are those who see that he was a god, but he is a god just as we are gods. I saw him grow up just as I grew up. I saw him do the same things that I did. Yes, his inside, his soul, it may be far advanced, but he was just a man. And I shared the things that we did. People want to place him on a pedestal when he asked specifically that the people not do this. He was a teacher, a lover, a man, just as I have been for all of these years. I've remained in the astral planes to help disciple people back to god, but people have forgotten who god

is by focusing more on who Christ is and I feel it is important to know our heavenly father, God..... To be with our heavenly father God and to not defer far too much from that when -- on my knees to pray.

Joe: Interesting.

Marisa: I am that I am that I am. Emanuel. I am that I am that I am. Inoculo. I am that I am that I am. He's saying "I am that I am that I am" -- .

Joe: Well God initially was the "I Am"....when...God presented himself in the burning bush to Moses in the Old Testament --.

Marisa: And people call me crazy.

Joe: You --?

Marisa: That was me, Marisa. And people call me crazy? Moses was talking to a burning bush?

Joe: He was. It's in the Bible. And God introduced himself as "I Am." And later on, people would say that Jesus would say "I Am that I Am".

Marisa: So...I am that I am?

Joe: Exactly. I am that I am. But people say it "I am that I am, I am that I am." And they would call him Emmanuel.

Marisa: Jesus?

Joe: Yeah. But Jesus didn't want to be called Emmanuel. I can't remember where in the New Testament it says that, but I think he said something like "No, Emmanuel is my brother in heaven," or something.

Marisa: Wait, hold on. Let me see who Emmanuel is. I want to see just out of curiosity. Calling in Emmanuel that Jesus – oh, okay. So you know how you have Noah, who's your seventh layer?

Joe: Uh-huh.

Marisa: Emmanuel is his seventh layer.

Joe: Is Jesus' seventh layer?

Marisa: Yeah. So it's his soul.

Joe: Oh, it's his soul. Okay.

Marisa: He says in fact he likes to be called that more, and when I see Christ come in, many times I'm seeing it coming through as Emmanuel.

Joe: Oh.

Marisa: He says that that's the name that he – oh, okay... Jesus says,

(Jesus) "As you speak to this piece of me, many times your mind –"

Marisa: He's talking about me.

(Jesus) " – will think, 'Am I really speaking to Jesus? Am I really speaking with Jesus?' And what you are speaking with as you are speaking with a piece of me that is within your mental body, for there is a piece of me within each one of your bodies, your mental body is the one that you spend the most time in. For many times you're channeling with your father, you spend much time in the mental body to almost filter us to make sure that nothing that will scare either one of you will come through. The most clearly you have channeled is when you don't speak of biblical things that can be disputed and

when you speak of things that you do not understand, so you do not know whether to filter them or not."

Marisa: Like just really abstract things. It's like I don't – I can't judge. He says,

(Jesus)   "So what we propose to you is that you place yourself within your heart. You place yourself within, within your heart and allow yourself to channel Emmanuel, allow yourself to channel the Christed energy in that which I am, for every one of us has a Christed body. Every one of us has a piece of us who is already excelled, who is already succeeded, who is already accomplished becoming Christ, for I, Jesus, was able to embody this Christed beingness within me for eight years of my earth life after my baptism. This is when I came into true alignment with the Christ body. So what I propose unto you is that you channel Emmanuel knowing Emmanuel is me. I am Emmanuel, he is me, and I am him, for we are the I Am."

Marisa: So his I Am presence, which I see right here, is also our Christ body, our divine self – oops, they need to get in here – and that's what he calls Emmanuel. Emmanuel also created –

Joe: Emmanuel was another incarnation of Christ then just as Jesus was another incarnation of Christ. It's like – it's like me going – after I pass away going back and meeting with Cesar Augustus or the blacksmith –

Marisa: Yeah.

Joe: They're all me because we –

Marisa: Yeah.

Joe: – all came from Big Joe, but we are all distinct.

Marisa: Emmanuel feels like a Big Joe. Emmanuel feels like a Big Emmanuel, and it feels like there's an Emmanuel and then Jesus, they're like separate, but Emmanuel is what is coming in as like the soul, like the higher self. So maybe there was another Emmanuel. I mean –

Joe: Again, that's all stuff we're going to find out when we talk to [untranslatable] –

Marisa: Yeah, exactly. I'm just trying to –

Joe: Let's focus on his –

Marisa: – understand what I'm seeing today, because it's different than I've ever seen before.

Joe: Oh, okay.

Marisa: And it's really interesting, because the energy of Emmanuel and Jesus…Jesus like molds into Emmanuel, like he melts into him, meaning he's a part of him.

Joe: Oh, okay.

Marisa: And that just makes me feel much more calm and at ease that I can actually call on something instead of just going, "Oh, it's Jesus' higher self," or "Oh, it's the Christ light." I can actually call on a name and actually get the correct being, because sometimes if you don't have a name for it, sometimes I'm scared that it's something different. So Jesus just gave me such peace of mind. I'm very happy. Thank you, Jesus.

Joe: I want to hear Jude's story. I want to hear more about his --.

Marisa P. Moris and Joseph P. Moris

Marisa: That's all he has to say.

Joe: That's it? Like his book in the Bible – short and to the point. You're leaving us hanging. You've thrown a curve ball at us, and now we're left hanging.

Marisa: He says "ask pointed questions" and he can answer, but there is so much to tell, but so little to tell.

Joe: Okay, let me ask questions then.

Marisa: Basically he's saying that everything that we believe is pretty much false. That the Bible is not true, that so many things were changed, that it's not authentic. But he knows that we're supposed to be supporting the Bible here, and that's why he's just kind of mute. Because he feels that he was short changed and the stuff that was written, it was changed. His book was changed. And then --.

Joe: But doesn't Jude realize, though, that 300 years after Christ Jesus, his brother Jesus, or his brother Yeshua, was here, that the story grew and it grew and it grew and it grew. You have to understand that. That it grew and it grew and it grew and it grew and it became a bigger and bigger and bigger movement and for that group with Constantine to take your words, Jude, as saying that Jesus was just a man with girlfriends, living a normal life like everybody else, would take him down off that pedestal. And they were trying to keep Jesus on that pedestal for what he did.

(Jude)   Which is why I say that it is not true. Which is why I say that many of the miracles, if those had not seen them, or I did not see them, I require proof that these happened. I saw others who created miracles just as my brother did. Those were not spoken of. For he taught us to utilize the Holy Spirit. He taught us to do these things that he was trained to do while he was gone. When he came back he taught us these things. We healed others. We taught others. We proclaimed to others what we

foresaw in their life to come. And these came true. And this is what he was taught when he went away.

Joe: Who taught him and where did he go? Where did he go, Jude? And who did he study under?

Marisa: *I'm getting India. I keep hearing Budapest.*

Joe: Buddha.

Marisa: *Maybe it's Buddha. Because I'm seeing like a temple with kind of like a Buddha, you know. But I can't tell if it's Hindu or Buddha. But it's got the gods, you know.*

Joe: *Well if Christ was Krishna in one of His incarnations, there would be a natural magnet for Christ and Jesus to go where he had once been before. And the Hindus were the first to proclaim the trinity.*

Marisa: *He says he left when he was --.*

(Jude) *He left for a total of 14 years but he would leave and come back. That he went and was trained in the martial arts; trained in breathing, trained in fasting, trained in controlling the human body through mind control, trained to keep calm in any situation, trained to be serene even in the largest of tragedies. He learned all of these things and taught us but many of the miracles, many of these things, were not explained or shown in the Bible, and this is what I felt needed to be told so that people of the world could understand that they could just as easily do the things that Jesus did, instead of looking at him as a god that must be worshiped, a god that would never have a sexual relationship, a god that would never need money or want money, a god that was not human. For, as this happens in the minds of human beings, it makes all of creation feel the way I felt my entire life.*

Marisa P. Moris and Joseph P. Moris

Marisa: ***Jesus says he was in India. It was a sect of – it was almost kind of like yoga type stuff he learned. It's – it was very Hinduish, not Buddha, but yeah, it feels very like India, but it doesn't feel like Hindu. It's not a religion. It's like meditation and prayer and breathing and going, "whew, whew, whew, whew," like breathing fire breath and pulling up energy up from the earth and calling in the Holy Spirit and expanding it out like the snow globe. So he learned how to work with energy in India.***

Joe: Well, I can say that the Hindu religion has been bastardized over the last 2,000 years, so I can imagine the Hindu 2,000 years ago is not the Hindu of today.

Marisa: Yeah, probably not.

Joe: Okay.

Joe: Which was...?

(Jude) Less than (human). And my mission that I embark upon is helping people to know that they are god inside, that they can accomplish whatever they want to accomplish, that they are in control of their destiny, and only that of our heavenly father knows our true fate and has control over who we become and where we go.

[Now he's doing this...a Namaste pose.]

Joe: Like in a meditative state?

Marisa: Mm-hm.

Joe: Waiting for us to ask the next question?

Marisa: I think so. It's almost like one of those robots, you know. You ask it a question and then it goes ...

Joe: Okay, then I'm going to assume then -- the story goes that he (Yeshua) grew up like any kid, he had the same desires. I'm going to guess though, because we've come to know him as being perfect, are you saying he was imperfect?

Marisa: Every human is imperfect.

Joe: Including Jesus?

(Jude) Including Jesus.

Joe: By imperfect, though, Jesus never --.

(Jude) I do not mean evil in any way. I do not mean bad in any way. I do not mean to say that I did not love him --.

Joe: But he had human desires?

(Jude) -- but he was human, and the Bible, as they call it these days, depicts that he was super-human. Yes, he was well-trained in healing, he was well-trained in the arts in which he presented to the world, and this was astonishing even to me, a highly unimpressible person, but understand what I am sharing is not out of not loving my brother, but loving humankind and helping them to understand that they are just as remarkable, just as astonishing as my dear brother became while incarnated on this fair earth planet of ours.

Joe: How was Jesus then after his baptism by his cousin John? By John the Baptist.

(Jude) Not much different, but people then saw him different. He was already respected, already looked up to, already had an air about him. He already had followers because he spoke of the ancient worlds, the esoteric mysteries of the mystery schools in which he was given access due to the stories that were told of his coming into this world. They were great teachers, great monks, great Tibetan mysteries unfolded upon

him due to their hope of reverence of this world by bringing such a marvelous soul into their teachings to teach what they knew, to pass on what they knew as the truth. For, he was trained in many things. And only after finding that the soul within each of us is just as strong as anyone else's because it carries the spark of the light, or as the Bible says, the Holy Spirit.

Joe: Well, Jesus recognized himself – and I'm pretty much paraphrasing the Bible – he recognized himself as the Son of Man and that he was the one that was foretold throughout the Old Testament primarily by the prophets. When did --? At what point did Jesus accept the fact that he was something more than just your human brother and was god? Because we look on Jesus as god.

(Jude) And I do not. I look at all "man" as god. I look at all man as god, powered by what is called the Holy Spirit, powered by an individual personality, or as you say, spirit, powered by a human mind that is embedded within the vehicle in which this individual personality resides in, and is in constant battle, so to speak, or constant resonance with the Holy Spirit or source that lies within. He began to believe the stories at age four, but never truly began to believe until he was told out loud by our heavenly Father god.

Joe: At his baptism?

(Jude) No (it was) prior to this at age 19. He was told upon a mountain and this voice came from nowhere so he had to believe. For he was told that he (is come) to teach the world that they are all --. "Ye are all gods." They can all do what they are taught to do. They can all heal. They can all be joyful. But in looking at somebody as if they are better, this does not give hope to many, although some may find hope from knowing that there is somebody judging them. But people find hope in knowing that they can be what somebody else sets an example to be. And that is why he was special.

Joe: When Jesus was told by the Father....was it the Father or the Holy Spirit? Was it the Father that spoke to him when he was 19 from nowhere? Was that the same Father that spoke to Moses, the I Am?

(Jude)   You can say that it was the same in essence, but the higher self of these individuals spoke. The true essence of them spoke to them. And as I say, each of us are gods. Therefore, each of our essences, or as you have called, higher selves, souls, are god, you may say that when one speaks with the essence in which they are, the Christed self in which they are, they are speaking to God.

Joe: Is this what Eden would call bringing – what's the term we used – physics?

Marisa: Oh, quantum physics into simple addition?

Joe: Yeah, is he really doing that?

(Jude)   Yes.

Joe: You said earlier that there are things you can't tell us because there is no way for us to understand. Give us a shot. Give us a shot here.

Marisa: I just wanted to say that Jesus keeps cutting in and says he was actually 17, almost 18 when he heard God's voice. Jude said he was 19. He was 17. It was before he went away, and that's what made him have faith in himself to be able to go away and learn all these – all these amazing abilities to heal and to pray and to – he says in my terms, "move energy" and help people. He was not on top of a huge mountain. He was on top of like a hill, like with sheep. And he heard... He says,

(Jesus)   "And I heard unto the ears in which I had in this vehicle, this vehicle that we call Jesus, and I heard unto

the words, 'I love you. I love you. I love you.' And at this time, God was vengeful. God would strike one down if they did not do what they needed to do, and unfortunately many people still believe this today. But the god that many believed in was a vengeful god, and when I heard the words unto my own ears, 'I love you,' I had a sense, a feeling over my entire body, a knowing within me that we are all God. God loves us unconditionally, and it was my job to bring unto those that I knew the compassion and love from God in whatever way God so chose for me."

Joe: Give us something that we wouldn't understand that would be a seed for us to move toward. Think of a science fiction writer in the 1900s who wrote about spaceships and everybody thought it was silly.

(Jude)   Well this is one of the things that I would speak of as other worldly things.

Joe: Being what? I didn't catch it.

(Jude)   For when we would see the night sky we would see those things that would come into the earth plane, and the communication between us and them was strong.

Joe: Physical beings?

(Jude)   The church feared the beings from other worlds and did not want anyone to know of them.

Joe: Even though they're hinted in the Book of Ezekiel when Ezekiel speaks of the lights in the sky?

(Jude)   They were not hinted, they were foretold. These were told and there are many, many beings from other worlds that we saw.

Marisa: [He just looked at me and he says, "You see them".]

Joe: We do?

Marisa: [He said that to me.]

Joe: Oh you see them?

Marisa: [Yeah, I see them.]

(Jude) So you can imagine as we see these things and we are told by them how the world will be, it begins to make us wonder who god truly is, or if we were under the impression that these were god, for they knew more information than us it was all quite confusing, and sharing these things with the world at that time would be quite ridiculous indeed.

Joe: Did the other disciples that followed Jesus and his ministry see beings from the other side?

(Jude) Yes.

Joe: In their dreams or visions or --?

(Jude) Not the other side...other planets.

Joe: Okay, from other planets. Did they see the physical beings, or did they communicate with them as Marisa's communicating with you right now?

(Jude) Both.

Joe: Both? So these beings that were coming from other planets were entering from, maybe, the fourth dimension back into the third dimension? Or were they coming from a third dimensional planet as well?

(Jude) We do not know exactly but the impression in which I received was they were bringing information to keep the world *on track in believing in one true god.*

Marisa: *So the higher self of Jude is saying,*

(Jude's Higher Self) "There are many pieces of us, many pieces of us that are fragment within the astral plane as both of you know; and many times, many times when channeling, some of those pieces will come forward. This was a piece of me that became very paranoid at times of other worldly things. Yes, we may have seen things at times. Yes, we may have even seen spaceships. We may have even seen beings from other worlds, but this is not something that is important to bring forward in understanding who I was as an individual, for it was only a one to two year obsession that he got on."

Joe: *Okay.*

Marisa: *So he says that – he doesn't want to be defined by it.*

Joe: *Okay. Let me keep going on this part, and then we'll figure out whether this – obviously this part needs to be taken out, but let me get through it, because we might touch on other things. Okay.*

Joe: *They were professing in keeping us on track?*

(Jude) Yes.

Joe: *So they are far more advanced, they have far more advanced understanding of god.*

Marisa: *Were they the ones that planned the whole Christ thing, Jude? What did they do? Stage the whole thing?*

Marisa: *He said he wouldn't go that far to say that, but he's just saying he's... Remember this is the Jude and we're plugging into his energy of when he was alive. But now I want to call on his higher self. Hold on.*

Joe: We're not going to be able to do James. Maybe James tomorrow night. This is fascinating. I'd really like to keep going with Jude but we do need to stop now--. I promised Jeff.

Marisa: Okay, well we'll just start earlier tomorrow. What time do I work tomorrow?

Joe: Jude, will you come back tomorrow?

(Jude) Absolutely.

Joe: Do you feel any vindication right now?

Marisa: Let's see. Tomorrow. I work from noon to 2:00 so we can meet --.

Joe: Well, I have that appointment at 5:00 in Valley Center and I'll be out of there by 6:30. I'll be over here by maybe about 7:30 and we can finish up with Jude and if James wants to jump in, but boy, I'm going to have a good time talking to Jesus about this whole thing with Jude. This is really, really fascinating. But I just remember Jesus saying don't put down the Bible, don't go negative or he's going to shut this all down. Is Jesus still here?

Marisa: Yeah, he's right here.

Joe: Can I ask him a question?

Marisa: Yeah.

Joe: Jesus, is it okay for what we're finding out from Jude? Is this okay with you? This is very different than what we learned in the Bible.

(Jesus) What he is saying ... you must take into account

that the aspect of him that you are speaking of, and speaking to, is what you could call a carbon copy of the personality in which he was while on the earth plane. For, the word "ignorance" would not be the word, but the unknowing, the unknowing that follows with speaking with a human personality at the time of their incarnation. There is much information that lies outside and within his knowing, but bringing in the personality of him at that time so that you could accomplish what you want to accomplish in getting to know these authors is what I have allowed into this room tonight. For, you are able to see my dear brother and talk to him indeed and see how it is that he thought. You cannot take everything that he says seriously. Take it as interesting and understanding what he truly believed. This is not to say that everything that he says is false, for much of it is true. But it is not all understood. I can clarify some things, but some things are best left to the imagination. For, where would the world be without imagination? It would not be in a very nice place. But there would also be much happier people at times. The people that worry about the future, their imaginations at the worst tell them how life will be, so they live their lives based on things that will never even happen. Jude has strong feelings about certain things, and I respect all of these. I respect all of these indeed. For, if I was in his shoes I would be searching for answers as well. I would be skeptical as well. I would not understand as well. And in this –What we mean to say, what we mean to say is that there are many depictions in many different ways of seeing things and this is the beauty of this book, this is the beauty of this book, my dear brother. Understand that as these different men and women come in and explain their viewpoints, their viewpoints of the same exact thing, you will see that life is truly just a perception. Life is not even a reality. Life is just a movie, so to speak. Life is not technically real. Life is not technically real. Life is the way that one would see it. Everybody sees life a completely different way. Even so, when people who read the Bible, when people who read these books, they see that all of the stories should be exactly the same, and the Church tried to make it this way to a certain extent, not wanting to ruffle any feathers, not wanting to change any minds about this, for the book was almost a -- as you would call "sales pitch," so to speak -- trying to explain a certain point, using the stories that all backed each other up. So just know that many that walked the walk with me, with all the others who were just as magnificent, just as talented, just as wonderful as the Holy Spirit instilled within me, they saw things that were quite different from what were placed in the Bible, so I have no opinion that is negative towards anybody who would like to speak of it. But when I say "do not discourage people from the Bible," I mean this when I speak to you two as authors. You may say that Jude felt this way, but it may or may not have been true. But it will just explain how a regular brother feels about his regular brother who is given the attention and the honor of a god, when everybody, everybody is god.

Joe: Is this Samuel allowing Jesus to come through clear?

Marisa: Yeah, ah-ha.

Joe: Okay, so Samuel's channeling Jesus at this point?

Marisa: Yeah.

Joe: And you're channeling Samuel?

Marisa: Yeah.

Joe: I wasn't sure if it was Samuel speaking, or whether it was Jesus finishing up.

Marisa: No, it was Jesus.

Joe: Boy, I hate to cut this one short, but we need to cut it short. Can we thank everybody for coming in on short notice tonight?

Marisa: Yeah. Let's write down where we need to leave off.

Marisa P. Moris and Joseph P. Moris

What are we going to leave off on? We left off on Jude and Jesus --.

Jude and Jesus

(Recorded the following night)

Marisa: Today is July 16, 2014. It's 10:05 p.m. Fifteen minutes before we usually start. And we're just going to do a couple hours session and wrap up with Jude and then call in John, right? James. And Jesus. I still don't know the difference between all these people. Okay, I'll just say a quick prayer. Thank you, God, for bringing us together. We come tonight to do this channeling session, calling in the authors of the New Testament, Jude, calling in Jesus, our guides, our angels, our teachers, all of which being for our highest and best good. I'd like to ask my guides Abraham and Jesus to act as a gatekeeper to make sure that nothing gets in that's not in 100% truth and 100% in the light of you, God. I'd like to ask Archangel Michael, Archangel Gabriel, Archangel Uriel, Raphael and Ezekiel to surround this room, to surround this house and protect us from any earthbound spirits, any entities, attachments, fragments, any dark energy. We ask you guys to please remove all of it, transmute it to light, and send any earthbound spirits back to their designated spot in the light. They're not welcome here. If there're any family members, loved ones or friends that want to enter the room, as long as you're for our highest and best good, you may enter. We ask that the light of Christ fill and surround this room, fill and surround our energy, on every level and every dimension, and protect us from that which is not of the light. Amen.

Marisa: **This is the new session that we're doing (Recorded 8-14-2016). Okay, so the whole perverted thing with Jude... I think I was just perceiving him like that, because he doesn't look like that to me anymore.**

Joe: Oh, okay.

Marisa: **He must have just looked really creepy to me, and I kept referring to him as the guy on Game of Thrones, and the guy on Game of Thrones is really perverted.**

Joe: Oh, okay.

Marisa: **So I must have been like imprinting the guy on that show –**

Joe: Into Jude.

Marisa: **– into Jude because – it looks like stuff may have happened to him when he was a kid. What Jude's saying is the energy that I was picking up on was some weird stuff that happened to him when he was a kid, when he was like six or seven. That's the energy that I was picking up on him, some weird sexual stuff. He said there was a neighboring village or something, and he used to go watch the people do sacrifice in the trees. And him and his friends would go over there, because they were really interested in, you know, just kind of like, "What are those people doing over there?" And they were told not to go over there, but when he was like six or seven, he went with some of the – one of the older kids and went over there, and it was like traumatizing for him, and he never really got over that they were a multi-god worshipping religion.**

Joe: Were they sacrificing humans or something?

Marisa: It was like sexual stuff.

Joe: Oh.

Marisa: Like they were doing stuff – yeah. He's not showing me probably because I don't want to see, but it was like – yeah, it was like – it looks like sacrificing animals and weird sexual rituals and stuff like that, and he was just totally traumatized by it, so he – it's one of the things that helped him to move forward in the one true god thing, because that was something that really shaped seeing almost like demonic-type stuff in humans when he was young. He was like – yeah, he was like six or something. But he says that there was a bunch of cults nearby, and everybody kind of practiced different religions when him and Jesus were young. That's probably true, right?

Joe: Yeah –

Marisa: If they were Jewish, doesn't mean everybody was.

Joe: No, no. As a matter of fact, Jesus condemned the Jews.

Marisa: Oh, he did?

Joe: Well, he condemned the leaders of the Jews. You know, calling them fakes, and he was having a lot of trouble converting...

Marisa: Converting to being Jewish?

Joe: No. Teaching. He was having a lot of trouble teaching the Jewish people, which he was one of.

Marisa: Born a Jewish person, but I don't think that he ever really like fully practiced it. This is me just looking at what they're showing me, because it's hard to channel him, because he's using names of religions and things that I can't understand. It's like in a different language, but he says... He says,

(Jesus)   Walking upon the earth at the time that I came was like walking through an orchard. When you walk through an orchard, you see an apple tree, you see an orange tree, you see grape vines, you see blueberries, you see raspberries, you see lime trees, lemon trees. You see all of these different types of trees. Are any of them the one true tree? No. Are any of them the one true fruit? No. If you take all of them, you may end up with a fruit salad. If you walk to one tree and you say, 'Oh, this orange is delicious. I'm just going to eat oranges for the rest of my life,' this is okay too, but does it mean that the one that's eating blueberries is wrong? No. It's nurturing. It's an – it's nurture – fruit from God and nurturing from God is like nurturing with food, nurturing with fruit. Nurturing is the god. It is not the fruit you eat in order to be nurtured. So what many did not understand and still do not understand, it is the compassion and the love that you feel from God that is God. It is not the Bible, it is not the Cross, it is not the Rosary, it is not the prayer rug, it is not the – it is not the yoga stances, it is not all of the things that people think they need in order to connect with God. It is the feeling and the nourishment that one receives from quote, "God" that is inside of them that is important. So when I came upon the earth, the earth was in great dismay in terms of religions. Many believed that they needed to kill in order for their god to forgive them. Many felt as if they needed to kill animals, others killed human beings, others had sexual sacrifices, others whipped themselves or hurt themselves to prove to God that they were unworthy so that God would love them. This is not nurturing. This is not. This is like walking into the orchard and taking a branch off the tree and whipping yourself with it and thinking that God loves you because of it. This is not the case. So many of us from this soul pod, many of us from this soul family in which all of us are a part of, began to enter onto the earth plane to bring a

message, a message of compassion, a message of love, a message of fruit, a message that when one feels nurtured, that is all that matters. When one feels the Light of God inside of them, that's all that matters. It does not matter what book, it does not matter which worshipping tools you use to get to this. It is just knowing and understanding that we are all compassionate loving beings inside of these human beasts, in essence, that we live in. Human beings have evolved a lot since I was last – since I was alive as Yeshua Ben Joseph. Human beings have risen on the conscious level in which they carry. They can understand a lot more. The mind understands science a lot more than it did prior to this time, for when I was alive, many did not understand science. We understood astronomy to a certain extent, but did not understand science. So the reason why this soul family, our soul family is entering back into the earth at this time is because science is going to begin to prove what Constantine and his advisors put into the Bible is wrong. Science is going to start to prove this wrong. So if we can come in and we can bring in the feeling and the nurturing of God, the nourishment of God so that all men and women on this planet can feel the nourishment of God, they will know what that is. You cannot watch a dirty movie, you cannot watch a horror movie, you cannot watch someone be hurt or abused, you cannot watch violence and feel the love of God inside of you. You may feel a perversion or an excitement if you have attachments, entity attachments, demonic attachments, even if your mind is perverted for the lack of a better word. You may feel an arousal of some sort when you see negativity, and this is just dark forces, whether it be within the mind or outside attachments. No one can legitimately and fully say that they feel the love of God when anything negative happens even if they despise the person that the negativity is happening to them. They will still feel some sort of sadness. They may displace it and feel sad for something else as opposed to the one – they will say, 'Oh, yes. They got what they deserved,' but then they will go and they will feel extra compassion for their wife, because their wife stubbed their toe, or their wife broke a dish, or something that is very menial like this, they will take the compassion that they had for this person that they supposedly are happy, something bad happened to and they'll place it upon someone that they adore and they love. So human beings must just understand that it's the nurturing of God that's important, and this is what we brought in at this time. There are many religions, many negative religions, many positive religions, but truly, truly what we are bringing was the one true God is compassion, is love, is unconditional love, and that one true God, one true God lived inside of me, is me and is all of you, my brothers and sisters in Christ, in God."

Joe: Wow. Still blows me away that you can do this.

Marisa: I Hope it's recorded. Good, yes, recorded.

Joe: It's recorded?

Marisa: Yeah.

Joe: Good. Okay. Let's see.

Marisa: Okay so Jesus is right here. There are my councilmembers over there as usual. And, Abraham, always standing in his same spot.

Joe: They're all so patient.

Marisa: Okay, all right. So Jude is standing over right in front of Abraham. He's actually right behind your head. Jesus is --. Yeah, he's like right behind you. Your arms are up like that and he's standing right behind you. And let's see. Jesus is here, and then I have my higher self right here.

Joe: Are you feeling your energies? Or are you physically

seeing them? Do you picture a real being, a real person?

Marisa: Yeah, yeah.

Joe: What does Jesus look like?

Marisa: Jesus is --. His face just came up really close. Jesus basically has like green/blue eyes that change different colors and they have, like, sparkles, almost like they swirl around. He's got trippy looking eyes. Almost like when people wear the color contacts, how bright they are? Almost like turquoise? They're so not real. His are kind of like that. He's got --. His eyes, he's got kind of big eyes. You know how Johnny has big eyes? Kind of like the Garfield eyes? But they're not, like, big where they're, like, open big. He has the little fold. Like the --. What is that? The German fold?

Joe: Oh, they fold down?

Marisa: Yeah, you know, like people --.

Joe: with....like bedroom type eyes.

Marisa: Yeah.

Joe: Bedroom eyes.

Marisa: So Jesus has like the big eyes that fold over and he's got his eyebrows are pretty prominent like thick kind of eyebrows. But not like, you know.... He's just good looking but he's got a square face. It's like high cheek bones that kind of stick out. But it comes down and then his chin is very angular. He has a beard. I'm trying to see what he looks like without the beard. His face looks more square with the beard. And without the beard his face is much thinner. And he looks pretty young.

Joe: Well, yeah, he died at the age of 32 or maybe 35.

Marisa: Yeah. He's not buff or anything. He's skinny. Kind of lanky and tall.

Joe: But Jude was taller. Supposedly.

Marisa: I just want to make sure this is really Jesus. Eden, can you say Jesus is my Lord and Savior?

(Eden)   "Jesus is my Lord and Savior."

Marisa: Yay! Abraham? "Yes". Okay, they all say that. I was told that if you ask them to say that, and they're negative then deceivers or entities will say something like "Yeah I know Jesus was a lord, yeah I know that he was a Christ," or --. But they won't say "Jesus is my Lord and Savior".

Joe: Yeah, even in the book of Jude, Jude said that the angels that have fallen are no longer in the grace and they're destined for darkness.

Marisa: Oh, he talks about fallen angels? I saw a fallen angel off in the corner.

Joe: Really?

Marisa: Yeah, it was interesting. I've never seen one before.

Joe: I think fallen angels have every right to be redeemed. It's their choice to remain fallen. It's their choice to follow the path they're in. If they don't like it, they can accept Jesus Christ as their Savior again....as their lord, their god.

Marisa: My higher self is saying that the fallen angels -- we call them fallen, they call themselves "risen" -- and they rule over planets and protect people, and promote free will to do whatever you want to do.

Joe: Yeah, but God lets us have free will anyway. (We) Can't be deceived by them. We've got to be really careful about who's talking to you right now.

Marisa: Oh, no, yeah, it's my higher self. No, that's in their eyes, what they think they're doing.

Joe: Oh, in their eyes?

Marisa: So it's not --. Yeah. Because you said they can be redeemed. And in their eyes --.

Joe: They're already redeemed?

Marisa: Yeah, they're risen, they're not fallen.

Joe: Oh I see, okay.

Marisa: They're looking at us like --.

Joe: They think they're doing the right thing.

Marisa: Yeah. They think that we're a bunch of drones, so they're trying to get as much people from the earth plane to join their side.

Joe: I'm sure they've got a lot of souls already.

Marisa: If we ask them if they're fallen angels they have to say that they are. If they are, they have to admit it.

Joe: In your visions, not human beings?

Marisa: I asked my higher self and others if he is a fallen angel? And they said, "No." And I said okay, good. All right, so Jude is here

Marisa: There's anti-Michaels and then there's anti-angels. That's what they call them, the anti – the anti – oh, my God. Anti-Christ. Oh, my God. That's what *** is, we see the seven Michaels, then we see five Anti-Michaels.**

Joe: Wow.

Marisa: And the five anti-Michaels are just kind of darker, and they have their own worlds, their own creations; and then the Michaels, which are of Christs, they look like Godheads, are part of creating souls with the Holy Spirit. That's interesting. So some of them just start off as anti-Christs, because there's got to be polarity.

Joe: Yeah? I guess.

Marisa: I mean – yeah. There's got to be – they got to set –

Joe: There has to be balance.

Marisa: There's got to be like a – like –

Joe: Yin and yang, black and white.

Marisa: Yeah, like a –

Joe: Right and wrong.

Marisa: Like they said to you, and they just use your golf example with Bill. They'll say, ask me to explain to the channel's father, life is like a game of golf.

Joe: Yeah, they've explained that.

Marisa: But they said, you know, who wants to go to the golf course without a sand trap?

Joe: There are golf courses that are very, very simple, but they're for beginners.

Marisa: Yeah, so that's why they're saying it is like that, "Who wants to play a game of golf like that more than a few times?" Then it's like, "Okay, time to have a little more excitement." So Peter says – Jesus says,

(Jesus)   *"My brother, you are a minister of truth just as I am, for we belong to the same soul family. And in this soul family, we bring truth, whether that truth is factual or that truth is an emotion or a feeling, this is where, this is where we begin to step into this world to bring the feeling and the knowing of truth. Many believe, but they feel deep down inside that it is not truth. This causes conflict within souls. This causes souls to not grow, for you have come as a minister of truth to bring to people an option, to bring to people an awareness; and if they believe, they believe, if they don't, they don't, but it at least plants seeds to bring people another option, because there are so many just as you have mentioned earlier, that we have mentioned prior, is 85 percent of Christians that say they believe do not believe, because they do not understand. So bringing to them an understanding is something that you truly desire, that we all desire, because this is the mission of our soul group was to bring – was to bring order to madness, was to bring human beings that kill each other for God or over God to an end so that all can understand that God is true compassion."*

Marisa: Cool. He just showed like 11 or 12 different lives where you're like – you're not fighting in an army for God. You're writing. You're like a scribe or you're studying and you're looking at the stars with him, and then you're over in the Vatican and you're scribing stuff.

Joe: I just think that our books are going to be written long after we're – or going to be read long after we're gone.

Marisa: Yeah.

Joe: I just do.

Marisa: I think so too.

Joe: Maybe as historical, because Lord knows what's going to happen, you know, as the years go on.

Marisa P. Moris and Joseph P. Moris

Marisa: Uh-huh.

Joe: But I just have a feeling that maybe a hundred years from now people are going to be sitting around going, "Wow, Jesus said that. Wow."

Marisa: Yeah.

Joe: You know, this is what people went through back then, you know?

Marisa: Yeah. Trying to –

Joe: Human beings trying to figure out who God is. I think there's no telling what the world's going to be like. To be honest with you, the way things are going, I have a feeling robots are going to be taking over the world.

Marisa: I keep thinking – well, they keep showing me 32 years from now, it's either going to be like enlightenment or –

Joe: I think robots are going to be taking over the world eventually killing humans. (NOTE: skip talk about robots).

Joe: Let's see if Jude is ready and make sure it's okay with Jesus. Make sure Jesus is in here, or Yeshua rather so he can moderate and make sure we're staying on the right path.

Marisa: Okay. All right so Jude --. Let's see here. Jude is here.

Joe: Is Jesus in here?

Marisa: Yeah, he's over there. I'm calling him in closer because --.

Joe: Jesus, if you're here, please surround us with our Snow

Globes, protect us from all evil forces, all fallen angels, anything that is not for our highest and best good. Please protect us from them. Keep them away from us so that what we learn is strictly from the light.

Marisa: It's cool. He's sending out rainbow colored light around the house. He's wearing white robes. It's like a bathrobe almost. With a gold rope tied around his waist.

Joe: Good.

Marisa: All right, so the room is clear. Thank you, Abraham, thank you. Abraham cleared it. Jesus -- you asked Jesus to clear the room and he cleared it. All right, so let's ask Jude some questions. And someone named Simon is here, but it's not Peter.

Joe: Well, one of the other disciples was a Simon also, but he didn't write a book, or a book that was put into the Bible.

Marisa: He's got blond hair --.

Joe: Oh, wait a minute. No, I think --. Ask him if he's Jude's brother, because I think one of Jesus' brother's name was Simon as well.

Marisa: Oh, really?

Joe: Yeah, ask him if he's Jesus and Jude's brother.

Marisa: I don't know now if I'm just making it up, but I feel like he said yes. Are you sure that Simon was one of their brothers? I don't want a deceiver in here.

Marisa: No. He said no. He's not his brother, the one that we're seeing.

Joe: Oh, okay.

Marisa P. Moris and Joseph P. Moris

Joe: Just ask for Jesus --. Look in the Bible and type in a request for Jesus' brothers and sisters. I think it's in the book of Matthew anyway. Didn't I read that?

Marisa: I don't know.

Joe: I mean, I can look it up.

Marisa: That's fine. This will --. "Brothers of Jesus. Simon, brother of Jesus. Simon was the brother of Jesus in the New Testament, implying that his mother was Mary and his other brothers were --."

Joe: Simon, Joseph, Daniel. Is that right? Simon, Joseph, Daniel, James, Jude?

Marisa: I feel like Jesus has --. I mean, you said they're half brothers and sisters, but it feels like Joseph had kids from someone else.

Joe: That's not in the Bible. They would never --- I wonder if Joseph was an older man.

Marisa: "Simon may be in the same person as Simian of Jerusalem. Simon a Zealot. Simon. Protestant interpreters usually take Simon to have been a half-brother of Jesus."

Joe: They're all half-brothers and sisters because Jesus did not come from the seed of Joseph.

Marisa: Yeah.

Joe: So all his brothers and sisters came from Mary. And they all came from Mary and Joseph except for Jesus. Jesus only came from Mary.

Marisa: Let's see. "Brother of Jesus". Simon was a brother of Jesus in the New Testament who has implied, has implied that his mother was Mary and his other brothers were James the Just --."

Joe: Yeah, we're going to talk to James.

Marisa: -- "James and Jude."

Marisa: And so James the Just, is the guy that goes, "ehum, ehum, ehum." [clearing of the throat sound]

Joe: Oh, okay.

Marisa: And then there's another James that comes in like a little kid, but it's a separate being from that James.

Joe: Yeah. We're going to get into that.

Marisa: The Simon guy... the Simon guy is just... he's not Peter. He's not a brother. Are you a brother of Jesus? "No."

Joe: Yeah, because you had – in the middle of this, of us talking, you stopped, typed into your computer –

Marisa: Yeah, but I'm looking to see –

Joe: – "brothers of Jesus," and this is what came up. "Simon was a brother of Jesus in the New Testament, who has implied, has implied that his mother was Mary and his other brothers were James the Just," and then you stopped. And then I come in and said, "Yeah, we're going to talk to James." And then you said, "Joses and Jude." J-o-s-e-s and Jude which I've changed now from Joses to James of course. And then I said, "No. Daniel?

Marisa P. Moris and Joseph P. Moris

Joe: No Daniel?

Marisa: It doesn't show Daniel. But, I mean --.

Joe: So, maybe he's not brought up in the Bible. But yeah, I think I remember there was a Simon that was Jesus' brother. Is there --.

Marisa: Okay, well I think he's here.

Joe: Good. Then let's talk to --. Let's finish up with Jude. Let's finish up with Jude, go to James, and then we'll talk to this Simon if we've got some time. See if he wants to add anything. So, okay, Jude, do you --. We've had time to think, Jude, about the things that you said yesterday. Some of it is somewhat disturbing because nobody wants to hear anything negative about Jesus. Not that you're speaking negatively about Jesus, but being realistic about who Jesus was as a boy, and as a man, as a teenager and a man. I guess the question of God --- In fact, let's skip that. I don't want to go to a question yet. Do you have anything else to say before I start asking more questions? Anything you want to add to what you've already told us yesterday?

Marisa: He says...

(Jude) You say disturbing. Life is disturbing. Life as a human being is disturbing and not understanding all that reality is makes the forthcoming of crossing over to this side almost disappointing. When you see that so much more can be understood while in the flesh, while on the earth plane you just want to understand more and this is how I was, and this is why I share this, and this is what I stand for. For there are aspects of me – (this is his higher self that just came in) -- there are aspects of me, there are aspects of me, indeed, that have muddled through the past, that have made it through, that have come to terms with the fact that this aspect of me, this aspect of me was angry, was upset, was scared, was ashamed of many things,

many things that I, he, did or thought or wanted to be. Please know and understand that this aspect of me is the human aspect of myself that you are speaking with. For, if this aspect of myself no longer exists in the spirit world, for when one crosses into the spirit plane, the human emotions are released. They are let go. But if you are to speak with me and recall my memories, they would not be of human emotion and you would not truly understand how it is that it was back in those days, back in those days, indeed. For understanding and knowing and seeing what the human aspect of myself was able to encounter, was able to see, what was behind writing the books in which were written, these letters that were written, these words that were written. There were many more words written than were published, and this is okay. For, there were many negative things written out of anger, out of resentment, but there were also very profound things written that were taken out, and because of this, this aspect of myself, this human version of myself, just as the two of you are human versions of your higher selves, you must understand that the human being will hang onto these things, will hang onto them indeed.

Joe: Okay, I think that can lead me into my first question unless he has anything else to add.

Marisa: He says...

(Jude) *My love for Jesus, my love for Christ, my love for the understanding of this side and that side is quite strong. Please do not be deferred from my love for God, my love for the Father. My devotion, my dedication, my ascension, my ability to transcend time and space in understanding and knowing that the human soul must ascend and must awaken, and must travel through incarnations as an awakened being prior to becoming Christed as my earth brother was able to become. One must become ascended first, and this is where I am. But this does not change the human incarnations in which I lived, for I was steps away from ascension and becoming an ascended master when in that lifetime. I have since then accomplished this goal.*

Joe: Wow. Wow. That's impressive.

(Jude) Three more lives after. Three more lives after the life in which I, Jude, am representing to you as my physical being. Three more lives were lived on the earth plane and then the ascension happened.

Joe: When was the last time you lived on earth? What year? What country?

Marisa: France. Italy. France and Italy. Traveled.

Joe: We'll say it again, you know, we choose what kind of people we're going to be. I've got some questions for Jude.

Marisa: Okay.

Joe: Any time he's ready.

Marisa: Yeah, they're ready.

Joe: Okay. The first question that comes to my mind is: one of the things that we've learned, Jude, is that people who condemn others tend to be looking in a mirror. They're really looking at themselves. They're really complaining about themselves. They want people to think (that) people who complain want people to think that they're wise, but in reality they're just pointing fingers at themselves. We've been taught this from the other side by many including Abraham, Eden, Delores, Jeremy, Samuel. I think all of them pretty much have told us that. But, in your book you're very judgmental in that you speak of the lasciviousness and living for the flesh and you mention in the times of Sodom and Gomorrah and unspeakable things, ungodly things that people do, and that they would never rise -- because of it they would never rise to the kingdom of heaven. That's kind of a paraphrasing of what I read. So, given that, were you a bad *person as a young man? Did you do the things that you eventually pointed fingers at? Not necessarily being a bad person because every human, as we've learned is basically born with evil because we are ego and we are mind.*

(Jude) I wouldn't call it evil. Evil is defined by man.

Marisa: That's right. They just said, "Not evil. Evil is what people call it." That was funny. They just said that.

Joe: Okay then, did you, when you were a young man, do any of the things that your book condemns others for?

(Jude) I cannot say that I did those things but I cannot say that the thoughts did not go through the mind. The thoughts are always the scariest. The thoughts that run through a man's mind, feeling as if one does not have control over their own mind, that is the work of the devil.

Joe: Interesting.

(Jude) When one is devoted to one person, to a woman, and then have consistent and continuance thoughts of others without control over this, this I believe is the work of the devil. This is the work of, as your guides say, you call them, negative entities, negative spirits. I call them all the devil, Satan.

Joe: So the devil and Satan is a generic term for negative forces? Not one particular being like Lucifer or --?

Marisa: Lucifer is one being. When I say "Satan, the devil" --. Hold on. Whenever we start talking about this stuff I'm always real careful about what's coming in.]

Joe: That's all right.

Marisa P. Moris and Joseph P. Moris

(Jude)   When I talk about these things I look upon the negative entities that you speak of --.

Marisa: [Hold on. He's saying no. Hold on.]

(Jude)   I do not look upon these things, for I do not want to see them or feel them or know them, but I know of them to be workers that work for that side. There are many beings that work for that side without knowing they work for that side. And those beings enforce the behaviors of the ego, of the human and reside within the energy of human beings which cause them to not live with love in their heart. So, yes, I battled my own demons. I battled my own fury. I battled my own anger, and I battled my own desires, but I would not admittedly say that I was a bad person per se. My attempt was to be a good man and in all honesty -- [His higher self just stepped in.] -- in all honesty (I) wanted to try to be like my brother.

Joe: Well, I could see his love for his brother in his writings. Of course, then again, he also told us yesterday that Constantine didn't edit it once or twice, or three or four, but maybe five times. For such a short book, it's only a page long. It's two pages long. For it to be edited five times. My gosh. Is there anything in your book, Jude, that you agree with? I mean, to me it's good. I like it.

(Jude)   If the book is two pages, in the scribblings that were left, and the books that were printed, judging by the size of the pages, if you say that my book is two pages, it was really 18.

Joe: Wow. You mean it would be 18 if all of it was printed in the size, type --?

(Jude)   That specific book yes. There are four other writings. You must understand that there are many things --- you must get out of the frame of mind that this book was created by God for God. It was not created for God or by God at all. It was created by man. And those of us, the holy men, who devoted, some who

devoted their entire lives, others who devoted the second half of their lives to God, saw this representation of God as something that was not authentic.

Joe: What representation?

(Jude)   -- And it saddened us. The stories that are told. The things that are said within the book, within the Bible.

Joe: The New Testament Bible or the whole Bible?

(Jude)   We experienced the New Testament of the Bible. We know that by seeing how the New Testament was written that the same thing in fact happened prior.

Joe: In the Old Testament?

(Jude)   Yes.

Joe: Who was editing the books of the Old Testament? Like this --.

(Jude)   These were stories passed down from tribesmen to clergymen of that time. These were stories passed down and told by mouth until they were written down. Many don't know where many of these stories, many of these books came from. They are ancient writings that we have been given access to. But many (are) indiscernible. Many of them (are) other-worldly.

Joe: Other worldly like --?

(Jude)   Extra-terrestrial.

Joe: Extra-terrestrials left writings, their own writings for man here to study?

(Jude)   There are many that are not discernable. Many of it cannot be read that have been found.

Joe: Are they currently found? I mean, do they --.

(Jude) Yes, there are societies and groups that have found these and have kept them secret.

Joe: Where are they --? Okay, if they're secret, I guess I'm not supposed to know, but, you know, I'm curious. Where are they? Are they in the United States? Canada? Africa? Middle East? Germany? England? France?

Marisa: It's so funny. I heard Kenya, but that's like in Ethiopia. That's like super poor, like --. Oh, it's Africa. That's nowhere near --.

Joe: Kenya's kind of out on the west. I'm sorry, east coast of Africa. About 1/3 of the way down if I remember right. Let me ask you this, Jude, and I'm sure I'm going to be mad at myself when I'm reading this, that I keep interrupting, you know, I never quite allow all these fabulous spirits to finish their thoughts and I interrupt them. Another question is: just judging by what we have learned from you, I kind of get the idea that you may have been a Gnostic. Christians abhor the Gnostics because the Gnostic writings like from the Dead Sea Scrolls don't always correspond to the New Testament...

Marisa: That's what Mary was.

Joe: She was a Gnostic?

Joe: I think those texts portray a different picture of Jesus, so they are considered blasphemous, yet they were written in your time. Were you considered a Gnostic? Would you in today's vernacular, be considered a Gnostic from your day?

(Jude)   I do not know the term. I am not truly familiar with the term. I believe I would be considered a Christian, a devout one; loyal to my God, loyal to my Father, loyal to my brother. But simply speaking, I would consider myself to be an understanding person of reality in that the church institution does not have to tell the people how to love their Father, how to love their brother, how to love their sister. And, if they do not love them, where will they go? I believe in faith. I believe in what our God calls the Holy Spirit. I believe in ascension, truth, peace. I do not so much believe in man-made institutionalized belief patterns and sets of rules. This is why I emphasize and over-emphasize the fact that when one looks at a man and says he has never had sex, he is a saint. Why does that make him a saint? What makes him bad for being with a woman? How does this take him away from God, when God gives us as Souls human bodies to live in? Why does this make a man bad? This is what is wrong with the world.

Marisa: This is not Jude. This is some earthbound spirit.

Joe: Oh, is it? Let's see.

Marisa: Okay. So this is a Jude fragment again, all of – when he started talking about the alien text and this and that?

Joe: Uh-huh.

Marisa: His higher self's way over there, and then he's got another piece of him that's like an adult self, he's got like this 16-year-old paranoid self that saw something in the sky and thinks that like – so I don't think that that's the best representation of him, are these things that he's talking about. Let me ask Jesus.

(Jesus)   Again on these occasions when channeling, you were going back and forth between a fragment of him and

between his actual spirit."

Marisa: *So his actual spirit stands here beside me, and he's holding him. This other piece is an emotional fragment of him that thinks he's him. So – when he's 16…..he does not know all that Jude would know. He only knows what Jude would know up to that point, and is answering your questions authentically as to what he believes. But this piece of him does not know that four years from the time that he is talking to you, he realized and saw within him what truth was and what truth was not, so when he was 20. Yeah, that's a different piece of him over there. It's like if we went to interview the 15 year-old Joe then he would be different from the 50 year old Joe because the 50 year old would know so much more than the 15 year old – But, now that we have the real Jude, the Jude that wrote his book, because a lot of this is me trying to figure out who I was channeling and what I'm channeling and what piece, and what that; and that stuff that I would never talk about anymore, because now I understand it. Because he's not a pervert. He saw something creepy and perverted when he was young. It feels like –*

Joe: *Well, we have a lot of Jesus coming up so he can clarify – and a lot of mention of the Snow Globe, so let's keep going. Okay, where was I?*

Marisa: *Oh, I knew it. I knew it. Mary Magdalene was a Gnostic too. Okay. That's what they were showing me, all the red coats were the Gnostics.*

Joe: *Oh.*

Marisa: *Yeah. And they were like magical, and Mary's mom was one of those, it looks like.*

(Jude) This is what is wrong with the world, indeed, for

when one begins to think they are bad because they think of these things in their mind, this lowers their vibration. This makes them feel guilty. This begins to attract negative energy. When a person begins to think they are bad, they begin to do bad things. So when I speak of Sodom and Gomorrah, there are a lot of people in those times that felt that they were bad, so they just went and they were bad, and continued to be bad, because they felt that there was no release for them. If the rules did not state and look poorly upon certain things, people would not think that they were bad. Therefore, they would not do bad things. This is my belief.

Joe: Makes sense. You do mention saints in your book in the Bible, in the book of Jude in the Bible that you wrote and got edited, you glorify the saints. You also glorify the Holy Ghost.

(Jude)   And this is one thing that I was going to mention earlier in that when I say that I am devoted to my Father, devoted to my brother, I am also devoted not as gods, but to those who act as guides to us souls while incarnated on the earth plane. I have heard you say that we have amnesia, but we do not have total amnesia. This is just an easy way to look at it from a human standpoint. Our spirit knows, our spirit remembers, our soul remembers, our soul knows. Everything inside of us knows who we are. But that peace inside of us cannot be heard over the mind chatter, over the humanness. So when one human can look at a saint and look at another soul that they look up to, that they can resemble, that they can model themselves after, this is when the human being allows his spirit to be itself, to be who it wants to be, and to allow its memories to come out. For you may feel as if you were born new in this lifetime, but nobody is born new. Everybody is born with baggage, with karma, with attachments, with relationship issues, with cords. Everything is born into each child and this is what attracts the lessons in life. This is how people are drawn together. Because in past lives, other lives, even parallel lives, occurrences happen and an energy is swapped, an energy is exchanged so that these two energies will

be brought back together in another lifetime to resolve this issue.

Marisa: You know who this is? This is Jude, but do you know where he's standing? He's standing right where Rosemary is standing, which means he's a piece of me. Let me ask Jesus. Jesus says yes, that my spirit was Jude. That's weird. Hold on.

Joe: Wow.

Marisa: He says...

(Jude) Your soul is the same as mine but not your spirit.

Joe: You always jump in to say something just before I'm going to read it.

Marisa: Oh, really?

Joe: Yeah.

Marisa: Oh, okay.

Joe: Because it says – it doesn't jump out of Jude, but it says, "my," and in parentheses "Marisa's" [then continues to read from the transcript]

Marisa: My (Marisa's) higher self just said:

(Marisa's higher self) What we'd like to explain is that from lifetime to lifetime, it is the same from year to year in your lifetime, so understand, Joe, that as you may have a cord attached to when you were 19 to 21 years old, this cord is attached to when you were hurt very badly, hurt very badly

*indeed, by a woman in your life (*that actually happened...this is Joe. My first wife along with our three-month old daughter ran off with another man when I was 21). *This cord may be cut but it is not forgotten. So when another occurrence in your life comes up that resembles this or makes you feel as if this may happen again, this cord comes back and begins to strum like a guitar. So this strumming cord then attracts to it other cords that are similar to it, like a magnet. It is up to a human being to realize "I am recreating my past and this is something that I need to stop," and ask us to remove the cord. Ask us to remove...*

Joe: I was just thinking; this is all in our Snow Globe book

Marisa: Uh-huh.

...the desire to recreate these things from the past. It is the same thing with spirit. It is the same thing with souls. It is the same thing coming into this life. If something resonates with something that happened in a past life, these cords may come back. These cords attach and a soul or a spirit begins to recreate what they created in a past life. And this can go on and on and on for what seems like eternity. And this is why it is so important to act as a catalyst on this planet by pulling in all of the energy you have scattered throughout, by cleansing this energy, by being aware of the spirit over the humanness.

(Jude's Higher Self) When Jude speaks here he speaks of his faith in the spirit world. He does not call it this but this is what it is called. He speaks of his faith in extra-terrestrials. He speaks of his faith in ascended masters and what he calls saints. He speaks of his faith in that which is outside of himself for at the time when he lived in this life in which you speak of, evil ran rampant throughout the planet, thereby influencing and causing human beings to do animalistic things that they were then told

were wrong. And this caused a crash in society. And only now is the earth recovering from all of this and trying to not recreate the past. For, many of the souls that are alive right now, many of the souls that are battling, that are at war over who god is, were the same souls that were battling over who god was back in the day.

Joe: That's an explanation of amnesia right there.

(Jude's Higher Self) So they began their lives and they picked up right where they left off. And this is how it works. So they will continue on over and over and over, fighting for the same cause, until they realize they are just a spirit fragment. They are just a piece of a being, of consciousness. And realize "I do not need to be stuck in these patterns. I can ascend." And once one ascends, they are free. They are free from incarnation. They are free to do what they would like to do. They can re-emerge with the higher self, or continue on to other worlds. Jude has done this. This is what he speaks of when he says he ascended. But this aspect that you speak of is the human form in which he was, which was really quite a nice soul, misunderstood, seedy at times, but thoroughly devoted to God and undevoted to himself, for he felt he was a bad person

Joe: Jude, we really appreciate this. I really, really appreciate it. We're spending more time on Jude, who is such a small, small character in the --.

Marisa: I'm sure that made him feel good.

Joe: I mean --.

Marisa: To his inferiority complex.

Joe: Well, he's got a book that's two pages long. John has the Book of John, and he's got John 1, John 2, John 3, plus he's got the Book of Revelation. So I mean here John is, not the brother of Jesus, and he's got five books. Paul's got 13 books, and *they're all long books.*

Marisa: Peter says, "And what does this say about truth? The ones that were closest to Jesus, the women that were closest to Jesus," he says, "those of us who were closest to Jesus, they (Constantine) didn't use their stuff."

Joe: I know.

Marisa: Because it was too – he says it was too magical. There was too much talk of reincarnation and sexual this and reincarnation that, and chakra this and chakra that, and energy and healing and vibration, and all the stuff that we talk about now. Interesting.

Joe: They've brought that up before. Yeah.

Joe: And Jude has two pages. So... I seriously can't ever remember Jude ever being brought up in services when I go to church.

Marisa: I've never really heard the name.

Joe: Well, it's so close to Judas, and Judas of course is so hated, and I'm thinking, if I get the okay from Jesus, I'd kind of like to talk to Judas.

Marisa: Judas?

Joe: Yeah, the one who betrayed Jesus.

Marisa: Didn't we already talk to him?

Joe: No, we talked to Paul. We went Paul, Matthew, Mark, Luke, Peter, now we're doing --.

Marisa P. Moris and Joseph P. Moris

Marisa: Who's the one that denied Jesus three times?

Joe: Peter.

Marisa: Oh okay. So that's the one I'm thinking of.

Joe: Yeah, we're going to have a lot more with Peter when we go back to read it.

Marisa: Because I remember Peter saying something about how that was his mind, or something like that, or --.

Joe: Oh, he was so ashamed, you know. But that was the human mind, and if I remember, Peter was saying something to the effect that that's the human mind and the natural human preservation instinct.

Marisa: Yeah.

Joe: You know, we try to preserve our lives and that's it, it's not beyond us to lie to protect ourselves. And in essence that's what Peter did and he was so ashamed. His human self was ashamed. But there was a reason for it all, because there was a lesson there. Okay, I've got one last question for Jude, but I want to ask Jesus first if I can ask this last question. So I'm going to pose it to Jesus first and tell Jesus what I want to ask. They already know. They already know what's inside my head before I even think it. So they already know what I'm going to want to ask Jude. The impression Jude left with us the other night, Jesus, was that you were as human as any other man and you had the same desires as any other young man would have, which was to love a woman. We were also given the impression that possibly you fathered human children. So, I wanted to ask Jude to clarify that, but if you think, Jesus, that I'm way out of bounds and this is something that would never end up going into our book anyway, or doesn't belong in our book, then I don't need the answer. But I'm curious, I guess. Did you ever love? Did you ever have human relations, physical human relations with the opposite sex?

Marisa: Let me make sure I have the right Jesus and not an alien Jesus.

Joe: Yeah, because the alien will go, "Oh yeah, man it was party time." That's not what I want to hear. Maybe it's best to call in Samuel.

Marisa: Yeah.

Joe: See if Samuel can go ahead and channel Jesus' answer to this. You know what? Let's back up for a second. I don't know if I want to know this answer. I don't want to diminish my opinion of Jesus in any way. And I'm not sure if that would. Then again, I'm not sure if it wouldn't.

Marisa: He says that he was in love with one woman, in love with one woman his entire life, that of course thoughts went through his mind. They were never acted upon. But he was told that he had to be a certain way, and he was that way.

Joe: Who told him?

Marisa: His parents, the teachers he had, the masters.

Joe: The masters? The human masters or --?

Marisa: Yes.

Joe: -- or masters from the other side?

Marisa: Human masters.

Joe: Okay, I've got a follow up question --.

Marisa: They taught him that in using the energies that would be used and expelled through physical contact with a woman, these energies could be used to heal, but yes, [this is Samuel talking]...

(Samuel)   ...he was in love with one woman his entire life and yes, there were physical relations, but this was what he saw as his soul mate, for every man and every woman deserve to be with the one that they love while on the earth plane. This is the whole reason for living. This is the whole reason for soul mates. This is the whole reason for souls merging together and becoming one. With the institutionalized churches on the earth plane, the best way to intimidate or make man or woman feel guilty is to attack the simple pleasures in life, which is loving another person and being with another person. On other planets and other worlds, this is not the case. In other planets and other worlds, there are no physical relations, for there is mind merging, soul merging, where two become one. But earth is one of the places where human beings are still animalistic in nature - --

Joe: That's understandable.

(Samuel)   --- and need this to recreate other human beings. In other worlds, in other dimensions, the beings are what you would think to be materialized, or harvested. There are many things in many worlds that we have seen that we can explain that you would not understand, but know that when this man Jude speaks of people being proud to have their one true love, people being proud to have an intimate relationship with their true love, this should not be something that is looked upon as evil. This should not be something that is looked upon as bad. And for man to impose this belief upon others is the work of the dark side. For, any imposing thoughts to make a human being feel evil is what he is trying to explain he believes to be the dark side at work.

Joe: I'm not sure if I follow that last statement --- I'm not sure who he's referring to --.

Marisa: It's not really the dark side. It's just dark emotions and feelings and judgment. It's not really like a being in the dark side. They have lots of corrections, but I'm letting you read the whole thing to make sure that they don't just say it.

Joe: Oh, okay.

Marisa: Samuel's talking about Jude saying that Jude says that when human beings come in and say "don't think these thoughts or you are evil, don't do these things or you are evil, don't do this and don't do that," Samuel is saying that Jude believes that to be the dark side coming in.

(Jesus)   In a sense between light and dark the egoic mind, the judgmental mind, the gluttonous mind, if we are speaking of light and dark, that would be darker than the light, so it depends on how you look at things. Human beings are quite interesting. The natural fetters that they have and come upon are quite amusing to us at times. But we are also souls, we are also consciousness. We have just far exceeded the conscious level that human beings on earth are at, at this time. But it is quite endearing to us to come and to help the future souls of our planet, for we view this almost as a training ground for the souls that will evolve and enter into our worlds, into our dimensions. For the souls have to start out somewhere. But to watch all of the planets where souls begin and carry a newer vibration than the older souls, it is quite interesting to us to study and watch as man claims to be god. Man plays the god role. Man finds a way to make another man not feel worthy of god. And to this we find quite interesting and stand back and watch as man gives his power away. But we encourage, and this we do unto this channel, to take back your power, take back the love, take back the god inside, understand and know that ye are all gods. And once one understands this, the soul is ignited, that as you say the Holy Spirit is ignited, and within that and that understanding,

man can be free, you can be free. For, every thought that goes through your mind is not your own thoughts. Thoughts that go through your mind are thoughts of others who are passing you by, other's energy who is in your energy field (seeping into your Show Globe) and others who are thinking about you. If they are thinking about you, their thought patterns go into your field. For, the mind that is in the human being does not always think the thoughts of its own. For, the mind, the mind is like a radar dish, satellite dish. It picks up other thoughts of other people. And if the mind is constantly thinking "If I think that I will be bad, even if I do not do it," this is what harms human beings and makes them feel poorly upon themselves. So, in reviewing and listening to your conversation with the man Jude, not the higher self of Jude but the man Jude, this is the summary in which we are giving.

Joe: Okay I will ask the question. You do not have to answer it. Does the Bible mention by name the person that you felt was your soul mate? And the person I'm thinking about is Mary Magdalene.

Marisa: It's Mary Magdalene.

Joe: It is Mary Magdalene?

Marisa: Yes.

Joe: So Seria* that was mentioned the other day, she was probably just a crush?

Marisa: Yeah, the Saracita or whatever. He says that was his first kind of like crush on a girl when he was 13. I think earlier they said he was 12, but I think he was – he was actually 13.

Joe: According to our other last session, there was --.

Marisa: Seraphina or something? Jude just said it.

Joe: Seraphina? Seria?

Marisa: Yeah. Mm-hm.

Joe: Oh, that would be --. Oh she was probably an Indian girl that he met along the way in his studies. Seria? That sounds like an Indian name.

Marisa: I just saw a girl with like a dot on her forehead.

Joe: Yeah, I bet you he got a crush on an Indian girl when he was studying, according to Jude he traveled for 17 years to learn, either learn from Buddha, or in the city of Budapest, but I don't think Budapest existed at that time. So, it was Mary Magdalene? Mary Magdalene was his soul mate?

Marisa: Yeah.

Joe: But he held himself back from procreating. But I'm going to guess --.

Marisa: He's not going to answer that question.

Joe: Good. Fine. Because I really don't want to know.

Marisa: He knows you don't want to know.

Joe: Good. But I could picture him holding her in his arms so tight, like they're one. I can't picture him kissing her, but I can picture them just squeezing each other so hard that neither one wanted to let go.

Marisa: Yeah, I see him protecting her and loving her.

Joe: Then let me ask Jesus this question: it must have just been brutal to be on that cross and to see his soul mate standing at the foot of the cross watching him die.

(Jesus)   I knew that time was endless, as did she, for we have lived lives together. Many, you see. For, as we evolve through time and continue to meet, life after life, time after time, the understanding was complete that this was what had to happen. For our uniting in that life in which we lived was to bring an understanding to her and to I, of what true healing, true devotion to God must be. For her soul's age at that time was just as old as I indeed, so we saw this as something that needed to happen, but yes the human emotions ran wild indeed, but understanding and knowing and having faith that this is not reality, this is not the true world, is what carried me through. For, I did not feel the wounds of the cross. For I had already projected myself out, projected myself out through speaking mantras in meditation indeed. Removing myself from physicality, you see.

Joe: When it was heard -- this is terrible because we're interspersing all of this interviewing with Jesus and I was going to save it all for the next book....

(Jesus)   It's fine.

Joe: But I want to ask him one question and then we'll wrap up. We're going to have to put James and Simon off until I come back, and I hope they aren't upset with us.

Marisa: They don't get upset.

Joe: And I forgot the last question I was going to ask.

Marisa: About being on the cross, about being, about feelings and emotions, about Mary Magdalene, about her watching him die.

Joe: Oh, no, no. I was going to ask --. Yeah. Is Mary Magdalene Christed? Is she an ascended master now? Is she still kind of at the same level as my spirit is? Is she reincarnated?

(Jesus)   *Mary Magdalene was an ascended master prior to living that life with me. She once lived as the wife of the founder of the Jewish faith, Abraham.*

Joe: Oh, that's right. She was Sarah.

(Jesus)   *She lived as Sarah. She carried the divine feminine energy that is required by any strong man on the earth plane; for the energies combine to create one. Each one living on the earth plane, each male energy, also carries female energy within, but the male energy is much stronger. It is like a yin and yang. So when the woman that carries (it) begins to enter into the man's life or field, it unites and creates a stronger force, creating a stronger man.*

Joe: In other words, a woman makes a man.

(Jesus)   *And a man makes a woman.*

Joe: And a man makes a woman. Cool. Makes sense.

(Jesus)   *But the divine feminine energy is required in the healing and mentoring and pastoring of a world entering into the divine feminine world. For the world has been, up until last year, the year has been in a masculine cycle, and it is now entered into the divine feminine. This is why people are becoming more intuitive. This is why people are moving into the sensitivities of feeling emotions and feelings that they did not feel before. And this has been a feeding ground for negative entities and spirits. In the higher dimensions, being able to influence man that did not feel before, into feeling certain things, thereby causing them to enter into survival mode, this divine feminine energy, bringing up emotions and feelings that man has not had before, either causes them to be more vindictive, more angry, more sad, or they travel in search of the polarity within. They reach for and look for that side of themselves that is intuitive, that does know, and find the right support for that, which is Christ, God, the Holy Spirit. So, yes, Mary Magdalene was --. [It's Simon speaking.*

Jesus speaking through Simon.] Mary Magdalene was an ascended master prior to that life. Many, many of the apostles, many of the quote/unquote "players" in the crucifixion, in the dramatic life of Jesus, were all predestined, pre-planned old souls that had lived many lives together that chose to enter onto the earth plane and change the world.

Joe: He sure did that. That's for sure.

(Simon/Jesus)   This was a plan. This was a play, so to speak. Everyone played their part and human beings somewhat did what they needed to do. They were told not to worship Jesus but they did anyway but that's okay.

Joe: Who was told not to worship Jesus? The apostles?

(Simon)   People.

Joe: Oh, people. But Jesus even would say that, too. He would say "Don't tell people, don't tell people" that he was the Christ.

Marisa: Oh yeah.

Joe: In the Bible it says he quietly tells the apostles "Don't tell the people I'm Christ." I guess he probably realized that people would want to stone him.

Marisa: He wanted to be looked at --. No, what he is saying is he wanted to be looked at as a teacher, as somebody that can be a mentor to others. A god is untouchable in people's eyes. God is something that a man will never be. But by being looked at as a master teacher, a master mentor, that puts people in the mindset that they can be just like him or better. And that's what his goal was. But it wasn't accomplished.

Joe: It was not accomplished?

(Simon)   Because people still worship him as opposed to

respecting his path and what he did ...

Joe: *That's not going to change.*

Marisa: *He says...*

(Simon) *... the Father, God the Father, the Holy Spirit can be worshiped. He was just a symbol of what being devoted to and inhabiting the Christ consciousness could be on the earth plane.*

Joe: *Well, let's wrap up with this final question, which is the thing we discussed earlier, we were discussing between us. I have a spirit that is within me that is my spirit, is part of my higher self, who has allowed himself to come down and be me, human, physical Joe here on earth. Was your spirit Christ? Or the Holy Ghost, the Holy Spirit?*

(Jesus) *My spirit was both. My spirit was both indeed. If you begin to understand the construct, the construct of the human soul, if you begin to understand the construct of this, you will see that all is one and one is all, just as many of the teachers have told you before. But understand and know that the resonance with the Holy Spirit, the resonance with the Christ consciousness, is something that every soul would like to have. Please know and understand that the Holy Spirit, so to speak, is the first physical catalyst of the god manifest. This is the first vehicle in which God consciousness traveled. This is the first vehicle in which this consciousness was able to enter into physicality in the lower dimensions. When one can begin to comprehend that the Holy Spirit is a vehicle in which a consciousness can travel, one will begin to fully understand how it works. For, one can look at a human being, a human being with a consciousness of its own, and say the Holy Spirit is within it. But if you look at it as a Holy Spirit is what it is all in, then it begins to make a little bit more sense. So if you look at the Holy Spirit as the vehicle in which the consciousness lives in or is born into, the consciousness continues to graduate, raise its vibration, become more like the Holy Spirit, and thereby becoming Christed it will be.*

Marisa: Oh, my God, it just clicked. It all just clicked.

Joe: It did?

Marisa: What Isabel and I discovered last week, we frickin channeled right here.

Joe: Really? Two years ago.

Marisa: *We're not the spirit, we're not the soul, we're not the Oversoul, we're not the Holy Spirit. The Holy Spirit is a vehicle just like the spirit's a vehicle, just like the soul's a vehicle, just like the Christ is a vehicle, just like God is a vehicle for our consciousness, which is the little silver dot with the GoPro video, and then the Holy Spirit puts a bubble around us and stamps us with the number. And then we get sent off to soul school, and they give us a soul suit, and they say, " Okay, go make a bunch of little spirits, and as you evolve through your chakras, your little soul suit will light up and all your chakras will light up," but we're not the soul suit either, and we're not the bubble. It's just the vehicle. We're the spark of God.*

Joe: Uh-huh.

Marisa: *We channeled it. I didn't get it –*

Joe: Two years ago?

Marisa: Yeah. But see what they're saying there, I could have never said now, because now I know too much.

Joe: Oh, okay.

Marisa: So the fact that they're saying look at the Holy

Spirit as a vehicle, so the Holy Spirit is within someone –

Joe: So if you look at the Holy Spirit as a vehicle –

Marisa: Wait. Read that again.

[Reading last sentence of transcript (copied and pasted)]

(Jesus)   So if you look at the Holy Spirit as the vehicle in which the consciousness lives in or is born into, the consciousness continues to graduate, raise its vibration, become more like the Holy Spirit, and thereby becoming Christed it will be. So it is that other way around that other people look at this. They look at it as an awakening, the Holy Spirit inside; whereas, we explain to you that the Holy Spirit is the vehicle in which souls are created. Now, one can choose to turn their back on God. One can choose to not want to enter into the light. But this never changes the fact that this soul was created by the Holy Spirit.

New Parable

Thereby look at the Holy Spirit as a little lining around the soul. It is a little lining around the soul and the soul is inside. You may look at one of your dog toys. The Holy Spirit is the fabric on the outside. The consciousness is the stuffing. And the squeaker inside is the human being...and the human mind.

Joe: I had a feeling that one was coming. I love his analogies. I love his parables. I love his metaphors.

(Jesus)   So look at the stuffing as continuing to build more and more stuffing, more stuffing with all of the things happening in that soul's life. It continues to build more and more stuffing until it is full, until it is Christed, until it has experienced all the stuffing it can possibly experience. And

therefore gets rid of the squeaker, so to speak, and it then is just the Holy Spirit with the Christed soul inside. And this is how the souls evolve. When they choose to enter back into a physical body, the soul surrounds the physical body and is within the physical body. It is not that the soul is a tiny small little thing within a physical body. <u>The soul carries the physical body inside of it as well.</u>

Joe: Oh it surrounds us?

Marisa: Yes.

Joe: It is sort of our Snow Globe!

Marisa: Yes.

(Jesus)   So when one is calling its soul into its heart and tuning into its soul, you may call it into your heart center to fully tune into the full capacity of the soul, but the soul is multidimensional. The soul travels through all time and space. The soul is much bigger than a physical being. A physical being is just one small, little layer of a being. So in answer to your question, each soul is already lined with the Holy Spirit. Each soul is capable of becoming Christ. Each soul can follow in the direction of those who have become like Christ in their lifetime, Jesus being the prime example...

Marisa: This is Samuel talking now...

(Samuel) ... Jesus being the prime example. And understanding how he did it. And this is loving your fellow man, understanding and not judging, and knowing that we are all the Holy Spirit. We are all god. And we all carry the consciousness that continues to evolve through time in order to become like Christ. And once one is like Christ, they have many choices and many worlds that they may want to go to, go to other dimensions. But for the most part, this is a graduation ceremony so to speak where the soul has accomplished its goal.

Joe: Perfect. We should wrap up on this point. But there's one question that maybe we don't need an answer to right now, but I'm going to ask it in the future when I'm sitting with Jesus and having a full-on interview for our next book. One of the main things that I hear in sermon after sermon after sermon after sermon in the church is the misunderstanding, or just the flat out not understanding, I don't even call it a misunderstanding, it's a not-understanding why Jesus said, "My god, my god, why have you forsaken me?" while you were on the cross. Granted, that comes from the 22nd Psalm and that was truly David when he was in the depths of his depression and going through all of his guilt, dealing with Bathsheba, and having her husband killed, etcetera, etcetera. He wrote a lot of songs, he wrote a lot of psalms, he wrote the 22nd Psalm where he said, "My god, my god, why have you forsaken me." But you, Jesus, on the cross said those words. And now all the pastors wonder why you said those words, especially when they think that you were God. They can never quite understand why you were praying to yourself if you were God. So they're totally confused on the trinity. And we'll get into that in another interview later.

(Jesus)   Because I'm not the one true God. We are all gods. And as I have just explained and you too understand now - --

Joe: And I understand it and you have explained that.

(Jesus)   --- for the human speaks with the spirit inside, but I can say that I did not say those words.

Joe: The other day when we were in a session it was one of the first things I was asking. "Why did you say those words on the cross? And – both of them had zippers across their mouths.

Marisa: Yup.

Joe: And they were looking at you, and they were looking at each other and then they were looking at you.

Marisa: And now I can actually see them. I couldn't see them at that time. Okay, so – wait. I was channeling before I started talking about the dog toy.

Joe: So you said this two years ago.

Marisa: I know. It's crazy. I am totally fascinated to hear what's on our first tapes. I bet there's so much good stuff, because my mind –

Joe: I'll bring them back from Puerto Vallarta.

Marisa: Yeah. Let's listen to them, because – because if you think about it, those first channeling sessions, when I'm talking about the Holy Spirit as a vehicle [untranslatable], and then I started channeling something else where I started molding it around – I think it was Samuel – I started molding it around what my brain knows, because he's in my energy. This Simon that's here is a teacher. Yeah. He's a guide. No. Simon is a – Simon doesn't feel like he was alive with them. He's standing next to Alpheus, which tells me he's a spirit guide. Were you alive, Simon? He says, no, he was not alive at that time. He says," In fact, this is what I really look like" ... and he took off his robes, and he looks like a great beam of light. So he comes in with blonde hair wearing a cross and robes. Were you Jesus' guide? "No." Jude's? He was Jude's guide. Yeah. He was just a guide. So that's why he's in here. He's almost like coming in to represent Jude since Jude is kind of like on another planet.

Joe: I think that we may have to interview Jude again but I like some of the stuff that Jesus' got in here. Let's just finish up here.

Marisa: I think that this book's going to be a really good one.

Joe: The Jude and James Book?

Marisa: I don't think it will come out for about a year or more. That's what I see. There was some stuff that you were just reading that I was waiting for you to – waiting to make sure you didn't mention it, but there was a lot of stuff that now I've forgotten, because now I'm like, "What the –" I forgot that, he was like, "Yeah, that's not right. That's not right. That's not right."

Joe: What was it about?

Marisa: Jesus and the girl, and it wasn't an Indian girl. It was a girl that they both liked from their hometown when Jude was young, and Jesus liked her too, but there was – did Jude and Jesus travel together?

Joe: We didn't ask them.

Marisa: Oh, okay, because I thought in there somewhere you had said they traveled for 17 years together –

Joe: No.

Marisa: – and they said that's not true.

Joe: Jesus went off on his own.

Marisa: Oh, okay.

Joe: They were his – you know, seven years younger, so –

Marisa: Yeah.

Joe: – he left him behind.

Marisa: Yeah. It feels like Jude and Jesus liked the same

girl. Jude was 12 or 13, Jesus was 19 or 20, but it was right before Jesus left. And Jesus left, and when he came back, it feels like that's when he met Mary.

Joe: Well, let's see. Questions might be answered in these next seven pages.

Marisa: No. He met Mary before. He knew of her.

Joe: Let's see.

Joe: You did not say those words? (Why God have you forsaken me?)...

(Jesus)   No.

Joe: ... so that was something dreamed up by --?

(Jesus)   I said a prayer. I was in a meditative state ... I said a prayer throughout a mantra; a mantra speaking of removing myself from the confines of the human vessel. Removing myself from the confines of the human vessel, whereby allowing myself to project from the human vessel, whereby understanding and seeing all of the things that were going on from afar. But these were mantras spoken of and taught to me in the secret mystery school that I attended, that I learned from, whereby the human mind and even the human body can be put into a state where it does not feel. For yes, I was human, just as you are human now, and yes I was going to miss my beloved, I was going to miss my friends, all for the knowing that this was all planned though. And I was shown that through dreams. And I was shown that. I knew what was to happen. But no one can ever quite prepare themselves for the agony and pain in which one can feel when they are being stricken and their flesh is being crushed.

Joe: It hurts thinking about it.

(Jesus) But understand that I saw this as so many other men before me and after me endured the same pain, so if I was to show that this is something that I would go through, it would make me just like man. I have been through so many things, done so many things as a spirit, as a soul, on many other planets, many other worlds, that this was a finale for me, so to speak, in learning and understanding the humility of being a human being, and learning and understanding and knowing that even when one feels like they are in complete control, they are never truly in complete control, for they have a mind, the human mind, that believes it is in control. And learning to master the human body is truly the greatest gift of all. Taking care of the human body; keeping the human body healthy; keeping it functioning is a way of honoring the God that created it, the Holy Spirit that resides around it. And this is something, something that many human beings have a hard time with. And this is something that I was able to experience in the human plane -- the temptations of ruining the body in which our spirit so faithfully is living in. And then to see other men ruin other's bodies and destroy them is quite heartbreaking, but something that my guide and I felt that I should experience.

Joe: Who's your guide?

Marisa: Yeshua.

Joe: No wonder we always get two Yeshuas in here. Yeshua the man Jesus, and Jesus had a guide by the name of Yeshua. No wonder we've had a couple of Yeshuas in here.

Marisa: Got it. Okay.

Joe: Okay, very, very last question and then we're going to wrap it up. As you expired on the cross, it is said that you said "It is finished" and those were your last words. Did you say those words?

(Jesus)   Yes.

Joe: *Does that mean then that this was your final trial, your final reincarnation?*

(Jesus)   When I said "It is finished," the -- I do not like to use the word charade or movie -- but the plan was set forth and the actors in this life played their parts.

Joe: *So it was like the curtain coming down at the end of the play?*

(Jesus)   Yes. Thereby, when that was finished, I exited from the physical plane. I was able to enter into the ethers and work from this side to establish, to establish a belief system within the human beings. For you must understand that prior to, prior to the guides, the angels, to our Heavenly Father, prior to the planning of my incarnation, human beings were even more savage than they are, and they were after, for no respect for fellow man, and a soul, a soul needed to enter into the earth plane to act as a catalyst for change. And I was chosen. For many others could have played the part, many others could have done this, but I was chosen and I did this with great joy. So when you ask if it was horrible dying on the cross, yes, from a human standpoint, but when I looked at the success and the changes that were about to take place in the consciousness of the planet, this is when I knew I had finished the goal.

Human beings did not react the way that we expected them to react. We expected them to egotistically believe that they could be everything that I learned to be, and begin to follow suit. Whereby instead they thought poorly of themselves and thought themselves unworthy that they could never do what it was that I did, thereby back peddling and back stepping in the human evolution. But we are so pleased as ascended masters on this side to look upon the human beings in beginning to understand, just as the two of you understand, that human beings can and will all be like Christ. And this is when we speak of the coming of Christ. This will be when the Christ consciousness reigns over the earth plane and everybody, everybody on the earth plane is Christed.

Joe: Well, that will be exciting. But that will be long after you and I have joined the other side.

Marisa: Ascended, not Christed.

Joe: Ascended?

Marisa: Ascended, not Christed.

Joe: Okay. Everybody on the earth plane is ascended, not Christed?

Marisa: Jesus, is that correct?

(Jesus) "No..."Christed." There're some planets where everybody is in their Christ body when all are – look at it like this...look at it like you have seven brains; you have an intellectual, you have an emotional, you have a mental thought body that isn't necessarily intellectual. It's more of a combination between who you are and your emotions and everything that you have lived in this life. So this is a different type of mental brain. Then you have your spirit's brain, your higher self's brain and your soul's brain. Your soul's brain would be your Christed self, the Christed self in this example. So understand that if everybody is Christed on this planet, there are technically only twelve souls on the planet. So if everybody had the exact same one of twelve of the same brains, everybody would know the exact same thing, they would be the exact same way, they would all come up with the exact same ideas and say, 'Ah, I had an epiphany,' and then another twelfth person down the street said, 'Ah, I had an epiphany,' and another one, 'Ah, I had an epiphany' All over the world everyone would come up with the same epiphany at the same time, because they are all tuned into the same Divine mind. So

it is really much more fascinating when we see all of these fractions of ourselves and fractions of ourselves where we are tuned into the lower minds, not because they are lower, but just because they are further away from the Divine mind, and give these minds the ability to tune into the Christ mind, this is a much more exciting life in the sense of when you are a soul looking down at all the creations in which you have created which are – which is this, this and you and this channel called the spirit. So if all the spirits on the planet are tuned into their Christ mind, then there are only twelve beings on the planet. And this is quite fascinating, indeed, and there are many planets where there is only one Divine mind. Everyone is tuned into God consciousness, not even Christ consciousness. They are tuned into God consciousness, so they are all, all feeding off of one mind, one mind and working in unison as one even though they are millions of beings. It is really quite fascinating to look at all the different planets and how this works and how this operates and see the beauty that lies within the earth plane, and that spirits can be individuals but still have access to all seven of their brains. This is really truly an amazing creation that many creator souls, or God as you want to call it, came up with in the multidimensional human being, because there are other human beings, there are other more animal-like creatures that are not multidimensional. They are just tuned into one mind, they act one way, and they do not have the free will. The intellectual mind, the ego and the emotions is what acts on – is what causes free will within each human being. And this is really, really fun to experience as a spirit to see how we have unlimited resources that we can pull from. We are God. We have all of the information that anyone on the planet has ever learned, ever read, ever experienced within our body, within our Snow Globe, within our Snow Globe, so to speak. We have all that information. We just don't know how to access it. So through prayer, through meditation, through raising up our awareness and our energy centers, each person on this planet does have the ability to tune into the knowledge that any other human being has because we, in essence, are all one in the end. We're just not tuned into it."

Marisa: That's fascinating.

Joe: Yeah. I need to listen to that again.

Marisa: I heard the end. I need to listen to it too. Let me see what time that was so I can write down the time. I don't think that this tape should even be transcribed. I think that you should – I'm not looking at the time on the clock right now –

Joe: No. I want the whole tape – I want the whole thing transcribed.

Marisa: Oh, really?

Joe: I want to reread this whole thing with our comments and their comments, otherwise I'm going to be lost.

Joe: Okay, Jude, thank you very much for coming tonight. Jesus, thank you so, so much, as always. Thank you, Samuel. Thank you, Abraham. Thank you, Eden, Simon. Thank you everyone that's here and who has protected and contributed to us tonight. So Jude, thank you so much. We'll get back to you again. James, we are sorry we didn't get to you tonight and Simon, we're sorry we didn't get to you this time. If Paul and Luke and John are here, we'll get to you, too. We will finish this all up. And then after we've got everything done, then I'll have Jesus wrap it all up and then we'll write the book. And I hope that you'll inspire for us and hope that others will read it and find truth in there that will help them in their lives.

Marisa: Jesus is saying...

At the end of the 2014 taping with Jude I mentioned that I

was going on a road trip through Mexico the next week with my now wife, Drucila. We were only dating at the time. I asked for Jesus to protect us from harm and we were fortunate to receive this new parable from him.

New Parable from Jesus

(Jesus) Life is like a strawberry, it is sweet, but if you do not know what it is, looking at it from the outside, you wonder what all the specks are on the outside. You wonder if you're supposed to eat the green thing on top. You wonder what it is. So you just go ahead and bite in, and that's when you see that life is sweet. So take life one day at a time, and understand that sometimes, something doesn't look the way that it is. And sometimes it's just taking that leap and understanding and knowing that there's sweetness inside, and that you may just have to avoid that green thing on top.

Joe: Love it, just love it. We're going to have so many of his examples and parables in the Ask Jesus book.

Marisa: He says ...

(Jesus) Enjoy life, know that life is sweet. Do not be afraid to enjoy it. Do not be afraid of judgment. Just do what you love and love the sweetness in life. For the only thing that brings strife between two people is not feeling as if they are sweet enough inside and trying to protect another from them, or protect themselves from another through a reflection of what they believe is a bad heart inside. So when two begin to protect themselves against others, each other, this is the only thing that

brings strife in human nature. This is the only thing. So please remember and know that this relationship that you Joe have with Dru is a sweet strawberry, a sweet strawberry indeed. And it must be respected as that. And know that a lifetime is a lifetime. No decisions need to be made at this time. No life altering changes need to be made. Look at this as fun. Look at this as something that you are enjoying, enjoying each other's time. You are enjoying each other's nature. You are enjoying each other and having a good time doing it. There is no pressure required and no need to make promises to last a lifetime. There is no need for any of this. Just enjoy and understand and know that the two of you are like strawberries and I love you and bless you and will be with you indeed. For the love that I carry is stronger than one can ever possibly imagine, and I carry this for the two of you.

Joe: Well, thanks Jesus, I really --. That was Jesus, right?

Marisa: Yeah.

Joe: Wow, thanks Jesus. I really appreciate it.

Marisa: Life is like a strawberry?

Joe: So cool. That is so cool.

Marisa: The green thing on top?

Joe: It is so cool.

Marisa: It is so funny. How does he think of that? I could never think of that.

Joe: Nobody could think of that.

Prologue to Jude

Includes some James, Rosemary, Christ and Muhammed

Recorded June 15, 2016

Marisa and I are really careful with our books. We don't just have a session with one of the Authors and then take it all as gospel. Once we transcribe the taped sessions and put the rough manuscript together for the book then we go back and read everything so that "they" can correct, add to or delete portions as sometimes someone pops in that shouldn't be with us. Most of the time these are what we call "hitchhikers". Hitchhikers are spirits of humans that haven't crossed over yet from the Astral Plane, the 4th dimension, to the 5th dimension which is truly heaven. In the 4th dimension these spirits just can't seem to let the earth go. They were humans who passed away but for whatever reason, feel that they have to stay close to earth. Many will call them ghosts and others just call them wayfaring spirits. In reality it doesn't mean that these entities are evil and in many cases they were perfectly decent human beings but they are not ready for the next step so they hang around.

Notwithstanding the foregoing, after writing the original transcript and then re-reading it and making the changes necessary, Marisa and I sat down one more time with Jude and Jesus of course just to get a final take. Some of the following could have been inserted into the previous chapters but again, this chapter is a clarification and addendum. We found it quite exciting, especially when we got to Muhammed but Jesus told us it isn't time yet to delve into Muhammed. A time in the future when Jesus says its okay then we'll have a quite extensive interview with the Muslim founder. We left a little in but this is mostly a recap of Jude with Rosemary and Jesus both adding their thoughts..

(Jude)   ....for what I was saying, what I was saying about my childhood is that I was different than most of the kids. You may have thought that I came through as bitter. You may have thought that I came through as jealous. It is not necessarily jealous, but when one is a bit different and they are in a human body and they are looked at a little different, this makes one seem sometimes a bit defensive if they do not have a tribe, so to speak, if they do not have people that they connect with very well. This was me. I felt a bit like a loner at times. So as I grew older and as I began to realize the abilities that I had –

Marisa: ....he's calling them abilities, because that's what I call them

(Jude)   – the spiritual gift or the spiritual enhancements that I had due to my connection with the Holy Spirit, with the spirit within, this is when my mother, grandmother, great grandmother began to teach of the gift, the gift of what we now call the Holy Spirit. When a human being

can connect with this piece of themselves or with this aspect of themselves, they can surely be happy. They can surely feel joy, but those who are riddled with lies, with shame, with guilt, it is as if their connection to the Holy Spirit is clogged, and this is what I spoke of in many of my writings. My writings were about allowing and incorporating in the Holy Spirit into everyday life, not just prayer, not just ceremony, not just 'I have God, and then I have life.' For when one can live with an intuitive nature –

Marisa: He's using the words "intuitive nature" because those are the words we use

(Jude)   --- intuitive nature, hearing, feeling and knowing that God is inside of them, this is when one can surely feel bliss, truly feel joy. For when you feel those tears of happiness, we have said unto you that this is the Holy Spirit. What it is is, yes, it is the Holy Spirit. It is a very high, high-level energy that makes the human body, the human mind, the human emotional body, weep; because it is such a high energy that the human mind, human body cannot handle it, in essence. So I like to teach more of the mystical teachings."

Marisa: He's saying if there was like a church that he would relate to the most, like right now, today, it would be like the Christian mystics.

Joe: I don't know what Christian mystics are.

Marisa: Either do I, but I'd imagine a Christian mystic would be someone who did tongues –

Joe: Oh.

Marisa: – spoken tongues and told prophecy. "Tongues is what is better understood as channeling the Holy Spirit.

Marisa P. Moris and Joseph P. Moris

Joe: Okay. Let me continue on with his life, because that's what our books are about, is getting to know who the men are. Okay, you say you started writing your letters to your friends based on your beliefs and understandings when you were 32 and that you were 7 or 8 years younger than Jesus. So if you're 32, Jesus was already dead for probably 5 years. Did you go out on a ministry after Jesus died? Okay, let me back up for a second. When Jesus came back, when he came back in spirit and presented himself to 500 people who witnessed his resurrection from the cross, did you ever see your brother in spirit after his human body had died?

(Jude)   Oh, absolutely, every day.

Joe: Oh, okay....every day?

(Jude)   Yes, every day.

Joe: Did he talk to you like we're talking to you right now?

(Jude)   Yes, the same way.

Joe: Okay. You said earlier on in our book – and I don't know if we're going to keep it in there because hopefully it's you, but we never know when somebody sneaks in – you said you were, in essence, kind of intimidated by Jesus because you were in his shadow. Is that the way you always felt? When did you feel like you were in his shadow? Or did you feel like you were in his shadow?

(Jude)   I did – I did feel like this at times, but you must understand that all of the teachings in which he was giving, all the teachings in which he was quote, unquote 'chosen for' were teachings that I already naturally knew how to do. So many people will say that spiritual gifts

will come with a bloodline, spiritual gifts will come passed down from generation to generation; and this is in essence true to a certain extent but not completely. Jesus was born with the abilities to connect with upper-dimensional realms in today's terms to connect with God, to connect with the Holy Spirit, to connect with his higher self, to connect with his soul, his oversoul. He was able to connect with these and have the gift of sight, for he was able to see these things within his mind. He also had the ability to connect with the spirit realm or the dead, and this is why many of the teachings in which he went forth with in the world were teaching against devious spirits, teaching against evil spirits. I have the same abilities, I have the same gifts, but I was not seen for this. I was just seen as his brother. Although I did feel a bit in the shadow, it wasn't because I wasn't a man or I wasn't him. It was because I felt that I could do all the things that he could do".

Joe: How did you get along with your brother, James?

(Jude) James was tough. James had a stiff upper lip. James acted like a father, even though we already had one. James was all about making sure that we were doing the right thing, that he was doing the right thing.

Marisa: *James was very surfaced is what he's showing like, "Oh, we need to look this way. We need to do that."*

Joe: Prideful.

Marisa: *Yes. Prideful. He wasn't real in tune with his spirit or the divine piece inside of him – and they're using my words in my head – but he's showing kind of like he wasn't – he was just very third-dimensional, which is normal, even for right now.*

Joe: Well, in the New Testament, they refer to James as "James the Just". In other words, the word "just" would be – well, in English, we've expanded that word to mean justice. So if James "the just" had *that moniker then I would guess that he was like a judge and then the judge would –*

Marisa: Well, that's why the judge comes in with those wigs on. Remember? That's what the judge is, the old school judges, they were – remember? The ehuh, ehuh, ehuh, (clearing of throat sound), the guy who has that wig and the judge's robes on.

Joe: The readers will learn more about that when we finish up with James in the second half of this book. A couple questions – let me – we'll talk to James, but you're the brother of James, so I'm trying to get some idea – and I'll ask James about you, so right now I want to ask you about James, because what we've got so far is that James had a scribe, so I'm going to guess that James was not real educated or did not want to write or did not like to write. Am I wrong there?

(Jude)   James was educated but not in what everyone now calls biblical teachings but we would call the mystical teachings. He was very like third-dimensional or just very like law-abiding ...

Joe: Like a human father?

Marisa: Yeah.

Joe: He was acting like a father.

Marisa: Yeah.

Joe: One of the stories that James gives us is the impression he was quote, unquote, "slow." In other words, he was a very kind person but possibly slow in mental development. And, he was a kind person, but it was James that witnessed Jesus healing the lamb. Remember when it was raining? And the shed had – they had like a little lean-to shed outside, and one of the sheep was sick?

Marisa: Okay. Well this is a different James. There's another James.

There's a James that's the older brother, and I see a younger James like a little 8-year-old boy. Let me see. Is this 8-year-old boy a fragment of that James? Oh, I may be seeing a fragment of that – of him as a boy. Yeah, he was very sweet as a boy and then he got stern.

Joe: *Oh, as he grew up.*

Marisa: *Yeah.*

Joe: *Because remember when James was a child, he saw Jesus –*

Marisa: *Yeah, Jesus healed the lamb when they were going to die in the storm or something.*

Joe: *Right. And James also said, "He never beat me. He was never mean to me." Jesus was never mean to James, and he never beat him, so we came up with the impression that he was kind of slow and a little sweet.*

Marisa: *He's very sweet and he was very genuine, very tender when he was young, and when – it looks like when the dad died... Is that when the dad died? I think one of Joseph's brothers came. Joseph had many brothers. Joseph's brothers or Mary's brothers. One of their uncles, whether it was Mary's brother or Joseph's brother came to help with the family.*

Joe: *Oh.*

Marisa: *And James was affected.*

Joe: *Is that true, James?*

Marisa: *Yeah, he says sort of.*

Joe: *Why were you affected?*

(James) It was just really hard." He says, "You look back and you think back to those times, because I've lived since then, and death was a normal thing, people getting killed was a normal thing, people dying of the flu was a normal thing, people dying in childbirth was a normal

thing. So as human beings, we were used to this almost, but our family was different. We were all affected by each other greatly."

Marisa: So it looks like Mark – is that Mary's brother? Joseph had a brother. He came in, tried to help with the family, and it felt like he abused them...Mary included. He was just like a – you know, not like sexual or anything, but like hitting.

Joe: Oh.

Marisa: Which wasn't like, you know, now it's like you'll get arrested, you'll go to jail if they spank their kids. Back then it was more like he was just very like heavy-handed, and that made James very much like "We have to do the right thing, otherwise we're going to get in trouble." And James became very focused less on being kind and nice to just making sure that he stayed out of trouble.

Joe: Okay. We'll get more into James. We still have to read his. I just wanted to get a little bit of a take from Jude on James, since he was just one step below James, and obviously James was the man of the family after Jesus left.

Marisa: Doesn't look like James was the man of the family when Jesus left. Feels like that's when maybe the brother came in.

Joe: The uncle came in?

Marisa: Yeah, the uncle came in.

Joe: Okay. Jude, did you ever go out on a ministry traveling to other cities, other countries, etcetera? Did you ever wish to go off and learn the mystics that your older brother, Jesus, had done when he went to India, or were you bound in by the family that you had and did you stay close to home?

(Jude)   I stayed home, stayed close to home.

Marisa: They're showing him like in a – you know, like a log cabin-looking thing with a chimney with the fire going, real homey looking. They're showing a lady having a child and she's screaming.

Joe: His wife?

Marisa: Nope. It's some lady, and she's in like a carriage or I don't know what she's in. And she comes in and looks like he's delivering the baby.

Joe: Was he sort of like a doctor, a community doctor or something?

Marisa: I guess you would call it like a –

Joe: Like a midwife guy?

Marisa: He's calling it like an energy doctor almost. He worked with energy. He did healing, he did chants and prayers and tongues and prophecies and things like that. He was known to be Jesus' brother and he was known to have these gifts or abilities, but –

Joe: So people sought him out after Jesus was gone?

Marisa: No, they sought him out even while Jesus was still alive.

Joe: While he was still alive, people sought him out?

Marisa: Uh-huh. Let me see. Was Jesus still alive? Oh, no, after Jesus was gone.

Joe: Okay, they sought him out. How long did you live?

Marisa: I just heard 42.

Joe: He passed away when he was 42?

Marisa: Uh-huh. You died when you were 42? "No." Older than 42? Oh, wait. No, not this spirit. Okay. The human being that was James – because we're talking to the spirit. He's like, "I left that body at 42." And another spirit came in –

Joe: No, we're talking about Jude.

Marisa: Yeah, that's what I meant. Jude. Oh, did I ask about James?

Joe: You just said we're talking about James.

Marisa: Oh, okay, no.

Joe: But we're talking about Jude.

Marisa: Jude? Okay, show me a card. Okay. So yeah, Jude was 42.

Joe: Forty-two. Okay. So I've got a pretty good idea of who he was. He was kind of a family man, had some special gifts which I'll write about. So really what I need at this point is I need a wrap up. Whatever Jude wants to tell us that we can incorporate into our book about him. What would you like the world to know about you, Jude?

(Jude)   Oh, there is so much information that I could bring unto you. There are so many things that I would like to say. I have incarnated since that life, and I have since made an imprint on the earth plane as you know it."

Joe: Are we speaking to your higher-self right now, or are we talking to –

Marisa: His higher-self right now.

Joe: Okay. We're talking to the higher-self of Jude right now.

Marisa: Yeah.

Joe: So Jude, your higher self is going to basically wrap up for us – about Jude, the human's life, and what Jude, the human, or Jude, the higher self wants to tell a 21st century world –

Marisa: Oh, I'm glad you asked that. I'm glad you asked that, because they were switching back and forth. So the one that we were talking to was like more of the human one. The one that we're talking to now is the higher-self.

Joe: Okay. What does Jude's higher-self want in our book to tell a 21st century world from a guy who was the brother of Jesus?

(Jude) I want the world to know, I want the world to know that each and every single one of you, each and every single one of you is special. Each and every one of you carry your own light. Yes, we all carry the light of God. Yes, we are all of the Father, as you say. But we all carry our own distinct individual fingerprint. We each have our own signature. Each with our own signature so to speak. And as this signature which we are, which travels through time, we make impressions on the worlds in which we live. We make impressions on the souls on which we live with. As we enter into each incarnation as a new soul or a new spirit living life as if we've never lived it before, there is a fear, there is a fear, because we are disconnected from that which we are, or we feel disconnected because we know that there is something that we are that is much greater than what we are told we are. What I would like the world to know is that you can have God inside of you. You can communicate with God. You can feel the Holy Spirit. You can be within, you can be the Holy Spirit. You can be anything that you would like to be without fear of condemnation. There are too many that believe that Christianity is something that was created by God but this was not created by God. This was created by man about a man who was not God. Those that are extraordinary, those that can do things that others cannot do and cannot explain with science will be worshipped and revered and many times killed upon the earth plane. For look at the two of you, the two of you many will worship and say, 'Oh, my goodness, I need to, I need to listen to them,' or 'I need to talk to them,' or 'I need to just be in their presence because they can talk to God,' or 'They can talk to the disciples,' or 'They can talk to the apostles.' And then there will also be many that want nothing to do with you.

Joe: Oh well, you can't please everyone I guess...

(Jude)   What many don't understand is that everyone has the ability to be within the Holy Spirit, to have the Holy Spirit within them, and this is what many of my writings were about. Many of my writings were about tuning into and being in alignment with the Holy Spirit inside each and every one of us. For this is our God-given right. Our God-given right to have the ability to control that which is around us, to control the energy around us and to live the life that we choose. There are many that condemn, there are many that judge, there are many that say that those who are into – those who believe in and incorporate mystical aspects into their life are those who snub their nose at God. What I want the world to know is that those that accept that God is inside of them and who appreciate their body, their mind, their spirit as something that was created by and developed by God for their divine soul to experience life in, this is something that is revered by God, because just as someone does not take care of something as much if it is given to them for free, if they have to give something in exchange for it, this is when someone takes a little bit more care of it. This is why God says, 'I give you the Holy Spirit. You are my consciousness, you have this vehicle that is the Holy Spirit, you are a soul, but I am going to make you plan the life. I'm going to make you chart it out. I'm going to make you responsible for this. This way the soul is vested – or invested in this. There is so much separation that goes into each lifetime that we live. It is very hard to show and explain through this channeler even through my words, the dynamism that goes into each human life. If I was to tell you that the two of you are living on two different planets right now, would you believe me? No you probably wouldn't because your human mind cannot grasp that.

Joe: No! That's not true. I would believe it now.

(Jude)   Okay, good, because you are. You're living in your own universes, you're living in your own worlds; and when you come together, your worlds collide, they come together. It is very hard to explain in linear terms, but each person, each snow globe is their own *universe, is their own reality, is their own feature film. So when you can begin to realize that you're not just an actor in the film, that you are also the creator, you are also the producer, you are also the film artist, you are also all of the actors in the film, because you created them, this is when you can take pride in your life; and this is when you do not fear the dark side, you do not fear being deceived, you do not fear any of this because you know how it feels, you know what feels good, you know what feels right, because you know that you have the power of God inside of you. And this is something that I taught, not in these terms, not in these words, to the people of the time in which I lived as Jude, but I brought understandings from other planets. I lived in many worlds, many places that were far more advanced than Earth, and I lived on Earth when Earth was more advanced than it is now. So I've traveled through many different planets, many different star systems, and I may be considered eccentric or a bit on the divine feminine energy, and this is why this channel reads the energy as being a little bit off, because she sees man and she feels woman. It is because in many, many census, many planets, there is no gender. In one of the planets in which I lived on many times is a planet without gender; for the bodies are, in essence, grown, and the souls incarnate into them. There are things that are beyond the wildest dreams, beyond the wildest science fiction movies that many human beings would never even begin to accept as being reality, but we have seen it all, been everywhere, been to all these places, and I would love to share about this. Jude, the man that I was, the man, the creation in which I planned, the creation in which I lived through on the earth plane was very infatuated with the extra-terrestrial, with the outer limits, with beings from other worlds, because he knew inside of him that he was, that he lived in other worlds. We'll allow him to pass on the words that he would like the world to know."*

Marisa: So Jude says, "Thank you." He says,

(Jude)   *I just want the world to know that God loves them, that they are loved, and that if they prayed to my brother and they think that my brother is God, then they're praying to God. If they're praying to God and they don't think my brother is God, then they're still praying to God. If they're praying to Jesus, and they don't believe that Jesus is*

Marisa P. Moris and Joseph P. Moris

God, then they are, in essence, praying to another spirit. So the intensity of the prayers, the intensity of the energy that comes in through prayer is much stronger when one is praying to what they truly believe is the highest frequency. This channel (Marisa) does not pray to Jesus. She talks to Jesus as if she knows Jesus. When she prays, she prays to God. Joe, when you pray, you go back and forth. You pray and you talk. You pray and you talk. There are many that are praying to something that they do not believe in, and then they are thinking that God let them down, which leads them to not believe in it just a little bit more until finally they just won't believe at all. And this world does not need and should not be a world of nonbelievers. This world needs to be a world of believers but a world of believers that know that they do not need another human being, my brother included, to get to God. All they need is themselves, all they need is themselves. I bless you two. I love the work you're doing. I would like to help. Please allow me to come in as you want me for I can help. I can help change the world."

Joe: Good. This should be the end, but I do have one more question for Jude, and it is in his book in the Bible. I just want to ask him this one thing, because it relates to what just happened in the news here a couple days ago. Jude, if you're following with what's going on in this world, the world is having a real problem, a real problem with radical Islamic terrorism. They believe in a Sharia law. They feel that they are justified by God –

(Jude)   The Islamic terrorists are worshipping a fallen ascended master that says he's a god. He's of the underworld. He's not quite where fallen angels would be, but he's an ascended master – almost ascended master."

Joe: It's not Muhammed is it, because Muhammed never claimed himself to be God.

Marisa: No. It's who I think Muhammed battled with – no, Muhammed actually talked to a legitimate source.

Joe: At some point, I'm going to want to talk to Muhammed.

Marisa: Muhammad's here.

Joe: He is?

Marisa: Yeah, he just came in.

Author's Note Regarding Muhammed

At this point Marisa and I had a very pointed conversation with Muhammed. We both found it extremely interesting. Muhammed is not the person that most believe him to be. I wanted very much to include our conversation with him but then I turned to Jesus and asked him if we could incorporate the conversation into this book at this time and his response was ABSOLUTELY NOT! He said in three years we can for we still have to complete our interviews with characters of the Old Testament first (I squeezed on my forehead at that point saying to myself "yipes…we still have a lot to do"). Nevertheless, I don't like to keep anyone from hanging but you'll have to believe me when I say you'll find our conversations, once printed, with Muhammed to be quite riveting.

Joe: Is Jesus still here?

Marisa: Yeah. He's standing right next to him (Muhammed). They're holding hands.

Joe: Jesus, can we put Muhammad's words into this James and Jude book?

Marisa: "Absolutely not," he said.

Joe: Don't put Muhammed in?

Marisa: Huh-huh.

Joe: Save it for some other time?

Marisa: Uh-huh. He said that will be in three years.

Joe: Okay.

Marisa: He says,

(Jesus) *"You can still continue to talk to him, because he gives you a better perspective of seeing another religion and seeing what's happened, and then you can begin to see your own religion through different eyes as opposed to seeing it from within it. So you can begin to see how things are as you say, "bastardized and convoluted," and then see your own religion and the way this has happened, and you can see that people are just people. People (in the world today) are angry, people are upset, people are sad, and this is why the teachings of the higher self or the Holy Spirit or the spirit or whatever you may want to call this, igniting the light within each human being is, oh, so important, because the more lights that are lit, the more lights that are ignited within each human being, the more light is brought to the planet, the more priests are brought to the planet, and this is when the planet will surely survive through the animalistic nature of eat, sleep, kill, mate.*

"We bless you, dear ones. We love you, and yes, we thank you, thank you for allowing different energies of different people to come through. We would like to bring other religious leaders to you so that you can get a broader perspective, because there are many, many that, yes, will hear and see and understand my words, but there are also others that we can affect by just hearing from many, many different types of gods."

Marisa: He's talking about all the different gods, like calling in like Zeus and like Poseidon, calling all the different gods, so people can kind of see a different perspective, all the ones from Greece and Rome and –

Joe: Well, you're going to have to keep me alive for an awful long time if you want to have all those books out there. Okay, are we done with Jude? Time for James? Should we get Rosemary's take on Jude now, or should we wait til tomorrow when we get into James? Because I need her take on James and Jude.

Marisa: She's not even here right now. Hold on.

Joe: Okay.

Marisa: She was scared of Muhammed.

Joe: Okay.

Marisa: Hold on, let me see. She's like, "Shhhh, shhh, shhh." She's over here going, "Shhh, shhh, shhh, shhh, shhh. He's really big. (in a whisper voice)" She says, (in a whisper voice.) "I'm not scared of him. I'm not scared of him. It's that Achbad guy"

(Authors note) We referenced a being named Achbad that was with Muhammed but again, we need to wait a few years before presenting the information we had. Nevertheless, I would liken this Achbad as something akin to Satan but not quite, but Rosemary doesn't like him.

Joe: Ooooh.

Marisa: He's standing right here. She says...

(Rosemary) Shh, shh. (in a whisper voice.) Don't move. Don't." She says, (in a whisper voice.) "He's not real." She says, (in a whisper voice) "He's a program. He's like a program or like a built thought pattern or something."

Joe: Oh.

Marisa: And Jesus just went over and went, pppshhhh.

Joe: Oh, he's probably a dark energy that envelops some within the Islamic faith.

Marisa: Uh-huh, that's what it is.

Joe: Ooooh.

Marisa: That's why Jude spit on it.

Joe: Ooooh. Wow.

Marisa: It's a morphic field, so it's like a –

Joe: I'd have to read this back, but I'm going to do what Jesus says. I'm not going to put it into the book. Okay.

Marisa: He says this will be a separate one.

Joe: Apparently Rosemary is here. Rosemary, do you want to give us a take now, or do you want to wait until tomorrow when we needed the take from you on Jude and James?

Marisa: She says she'll take anytime

Joe: Okay. Bring Rosemary back.

Marisa: Okay. So here's Rosemary. All right, Rosemary, come over here. I want to see Rosemary. I love your personality, but I want to see what you really look like. Okay, you're really old. All right.

Joe: But she makes herself out like a valley girl.

Marisa: She looks really young, and she looks really pretty. She says, "I'm you." Well, why do you come in over here on this side? She says... She says, "There's 56 levels of the fifth dimension."

Joe: No. We don't want to go there.

Marisa: No. She's just showing me.

Joe: I know. We don't want –

Marisa: She says, "I'm at the highest level..."

Joe: No, no, no, no, no. I don't want to – I don't want to go –

Marisa: No. I want to know. Before I let her in, I want to know.

Marisa P. Moris and Joseph P. Moris

Joe: All right.

Marisa: I want to understand why. Okay. So she's just there. She's here for this purpose. She's here to help us.

Joe: Yeah. She said she stayed on the earth plane, because she likes religions and she likes teaching and so –

Marisa: Yeah.

Joe: – that's what she's told us before. Okay. Straight up, this could be very quick. Did you know Jude?

(Rosemary)   "No."

Joe: Then we're done. We're done.

Marisa: She says, "But I can tell you all about him."

Joe: Well, then, why? That would be second hand. If you didn't know him, then you're going to give us second-hand information, second-hand –

(Rosemary)   We can watch all the tapes from here. We can watch all the tapes. We can live as whoever we want to live as. We can go into a seat the way that you would look at it as a seat and look at a movie, and we can jump into any character that we want, so I could be him if I wanted to where I'm standing at right now. So I'll just tell you that he was a very nice person, but he was misunderstood. There are many that didn't really truly get him. For the use of this channel's words he wasn't very grounded. So many times he was talking about things that nobody really understood, and he just assumed that they understood, but he was very gifted, very talented healer, and what Mary told me was that she protected him from the world. It's like Mary taught him everything she knew – Mother Mary – and then said, 'But one of my sons that's this gifted has to live a normal life.' So it's like he had babies and a family and worked and had his little healing practice or something where people would come to him and he would heal them, but he wasn't out all

over the world doing ministry, traveling until after Jesus died. Yeah, she said he was a good person all around.

Joe: So in the – kind of in the beginning of the book, the impression we got, Marisa got, was that he had like pervy energy...

Marisa: She says he's soft.

Joe: Okay. So because he was soft, then he was probably thought of to be someone –

Marisa: She says...

(Rosemary) In this world, in this 21st century world he would be considered bisexual."

Joe: He would be bisexual?

Marisa: Uh-huh.

Joe: Okay.

Marisa: She says, "I'll share this." And he (Jude) was like, "Really!!!???" And he looked at her and she was like, "Well, they asked." He would be one of those that was at Sodom and Gomorrah.

Joe: Oh. So like when we point fingers in the mirror?

Marisa: Uh-huh.

Joe: When we see our own snow globes, then is that why he wrote what he wrote?

Marisa: Uh-huh.

Joe: So he's talking about the perversion –

Marisa: He's talking about himself, yeah.

Joe: – the sexual immorality and perversion, he was judging himself.

Marisa: He was judging himself.

Joe: Oh, okay.

Marisa: But he never acted it out. Once it feels like, almost but he was Jesus' brother and...

Joe: Yeah, so he couldn't do that.

Marisa: But he says that – he says that the cult or the religion that they came from was very open sexually, and it wasn't necessarily like man man or woman woman, that that – it was very like open, and it –

Joe: In the vein of Sodom and Gomorrah [untranslatable] –

Marisa: Not Sodom and Gomorrah. The religion that he was raised in, like it was very like female dominant, healers, prophecy, channeling, tongues, but that they weren't like anti-sex the way that the church is.

Joe: Oh okay.

Marisa: So he says that may be why I felt the weird energy.

Joe: We're going to eventually be doing the Old Testament, so we'll get into talking to Moses and to Daniel and to Joshua and many of the Prophets. Talking to Solomon and David should be fun –

Marisa: Oh, no, here comes –

Joe: No, no, no. I don't want the ghetto Moses.

Marisa: I know. He just came in. He says, "Yay, boy!"

Joe: No, no, no.

Marisa: Oh, my God.

Joe: Okay. Thank you, Rosemary. I really appreciate it.

Marisa: She says, "Thank you for letting me talk. You didn't forget about me this time."

Joe: No. We need you tomorrow also.

Marisa: She says, "I'll be here. I'll be here early."

Joe: Okay. All right. That's done. We're done for today.

Marisa: Okay. Yay.

[End of transcription}

James

This book on James was a little tough to do. This chapter was supposed to be just a straight forward interview of James, the brother of Jesus. The world understands that James wrote the book of James in the Bible but we're finding out that it didn't exactly turn out that way.

As we have been preparing this book I've learned a great deal about the reality of what was going on over 2000 years ago as opposed to what the supposed "truth" is. We learn in this chapter that James, the brother of Jesus, was not the author of the book of his name. We find out that the "author" is actually a scribe from the time of Constantine who was given a task to compile many works into a single book. If you read the book of James in the Bible, you'll find it to be basically a set of daily human lessons. I would guess this is what was gleaned from numerous writings in that time.

We know that Constantine's council met to put a "book" together for Christians in the 300's AD but the scribe you'll meet in the foregoing pages, who doesn't like being called a scribe, mentions a date in the 200's AD so we're really not quite sure what the absolute correct date is for the commencement of the book of James. For all we know and as you learn, this author of the book of James may have been born in the 200's and that is why the date in the 260's comes up. At times throughout this book I was curious to find out from Jesus and others whether it would be wise to mention or even give Judas a chapter. Obviously Judas was not one of the books of the Bible but then again, neither was Rosemary who was first featured in the Matthew and Mark book and yet we have interviewed Rosemary quite extensively throughout our interviews with the Authors due to her "objectivity". Rosemary didn't like Judas for what he did to Jesus and she labels him a "liar". Nonetheless, we do have a little bit of Judas in here as Jesus felt that we should speak to him, even if only briefly, to see what his mindset was.

There is a lot of back and forth between Marisa and I while trying to figure out just who this author is and just who "James the Just" was. I would have normally removed a lot of this banter so that we could get right to the point, but by leaving it in, the reader will get a better idea of what we were having to deal with to put this chapter on James together. So my apologies right up front for what might be considered some useless or distracting dialogue, but again, I don't think it is useless. It allows the reader to feel as if they are right there with us while interviewing these monumental characters.

So, with no further ado, here is what we came up with for the book of James.

Joe: (finishing our opening prayer as the recorder was turned on just a tad late).......Protect us from any darkness creeping in. Let the light shine down from above, and bring the Holy Spirit in with us, and Jesus as well.

Marisa: There's the Holy Spirit.

Joe: First thing, if Jesus is here, I'd like to ask him if it's okay if we talk to his brother James now, if he's willing to come in. And then also, he did say that Judas was an integral part of the story and that we should interview him. So I want to ask him again if that's the case --.

Marisa: Why did someone just say Judas is a liar? He has a knife. Why does he have a knife?

Joe: Judas was a liar?

Marisa P. Moris and Joseph P. Moris

Marisa: No, I just heard someone scream out from back there, "Judas is a liar!"

Marisa: It was Rosemary.

Joe: Well, of course he was a liar. To --where's the word I'm looking for? I can't come up with the right words—the knife might symbolize the fact that Judas was a backstabber to Jesus.

Joe: That's probably why you first saw –

Marisa: Looks like he's holding the knife, yeah.

Joe: A backstabber.

Marisa: Okay, yeah. Now he just dropped the knife, and he goes, "Hey, I need to use my props."

Joe: Okay.

Marisa: Oh, okay. It was Rosemary. Way off in the distance. "Judas is a liar."

Marisa: She's so mad right now. She does not like Judas, that's for sure.

Joe: Does that mean he's going to lie from the other side? He's not going to tell us the truth?

Marisa: No, no. I just heard someone yell that. Let me see. Okay, so we've got Rosemary here also.

Joe: We've got Rosemary in our book already.

Marisa: I'm just saying who I'm seeing here. So we've got Rosemary --.

Joe: Rosemary brings humor and levity.

Marisa: Rosemary is like in the -- I realize now -- Rosemary is like --. She's not earthbound but she's not --. She's still Rosemary. She's not like --.

Joe: But she's also, isn't she Delores?

Marisa: Yeah, she's just --. They just like you.

Joe: Oh, wow. That's embarrassing.

Marisa: I mean she's Delores and Rosemary. Delores was your wife in another life, right? But she just wants to help us here. Plus, she followed Jesus around and thought he was dreamy. But she's kind of like this lovesick, like, schoolgirl, kind of. But just thinks that it's really --she's just --yeah. She's here for commentary.

Marisa: She just went like this. She went, "Mmm, I'm not lovesick." And there's like steam coming out of her ears. She says, "I am not –"

Joe: Well, don't worry. We're going to get Rosemary on this later.

Marisa: She's just joking around. She's like hopping around all over the place. She's so excited. Okay.

Joe: Well, that's good. Well, we've spoken to Rosemary. If she needs to pop in, tonight, that's fine, because she can give us --In fact I like --.

Marisa: She's standing next to John. But that's not John.

Joe: I like when she comes in and gives us a little bit of a different take on the authors.

Marisa: She says, "This isn't 'John' John. This is my John."

Joe: Yeah but we've already spoken to John. And we'll talk to John again.

Marisa: She's standing next to John. No, I'm just telling you who's in here. So it's her, someone named John, and then I've got Matthew right here, I've got Luke over here in his, like, monk's robe, with the blond hair, I've got the guy with the crippled hand --.

Joe: Paul.

Marisa: --right in front of me. Then I've got my guide Samuel, who's right here. He's huge compared to all of them. And then Jesus right in front of me. And then Abraham right behind Jesus. And then Eden is always over, next to you. But if I was to call Eden into my energy, she'd be like way up there by the council. So anyways, and the council is here. Okay --.

Joe: But James isn't here. Ask Jesus if --.

Marisa: They're calling him. He's --. Oh, goodness. That was Rosemary. She said, "Oh goodness." Somebody just walked in and he went, "Er, er, erm." And he scrolled out this long scroll.

Joe: Wait a minute. There are two James.

Marisa: The James that just came in is rolling out the long scroll, like he's ready to talk and dictate it.

Joe: But there's two James in the New Testament. One is an apostle.

Marisa: Is one of them a scholar?

Joe: Wait a minute. There was James – he was the first apostle that was martyred and he was the brother of John the Apostle, not John the Baptist--.

Marisa: It's not him. The guy that's here right now is not him. That's not him.

Joe: James --.

Marisa: The one that you said is martyred, I see a guy that kind of has, like, his arms like tied behind his back, and he's like being pushed off. But this James that is right here, that is not the same James. This James has a long scroll of paper and he just scrolled it out like he's ready to read from it or something.

Joe: Well, hang on for a second. Andrew and Peter -- who was also named Simon -- Simon and Andrew were brothers. They were apostles. And then John and James were brothers. And James was martyred; the first one that died for Christ, the first apostle that died for Christ. But now I'm confused because I'm not --. The book of James I thought was Jesus' brother--.

Marisa: It's not written by -- it wasn't written by him?

Joe: --but he wasn't an apostle. John's brother James was an apostle.

Marisa: Well, this guy --.

Joe: So I need to find out, the book of James --.

Marisa: Who was the book of James written by?

Joe: I think we've got --. I need to find out if the James who is the author was Jesus' brother, or was it John's brother, because they were called the Sons of Thunder. John and James were the Sons of Thunder, and they were brothers. But there is an author, and then Jesus' eldest brother, the one that was born after him, his name is James. I think the author of the book of James was Jesus' brother. I think. We need to ask Jesus. But James, the apostle, who was John's brother, is the one who was – political...he wanted to fight. He was like a warrior. And he was --*anybody who would speak out against Jesus or anybody else, James would be ready to go kill them. In fact, I think it was James that cut off --. When the Romans came to arrest Jesus, James cut the ear off of one of the Roman centurions. And that's when Jesus stopped him and said, 'No, that's not the way to prove a point. We're not going to be killing people, and we're not going to be fighting.' But eventually, James, the brother of John was killed. He was killed standing up for Jesus. So I think the James that was killed was not an author of one of the books of the Bible.*

Marisa: *Well, this guy that I'm seeing, the James that is standing right here in front of me, I don't know who he is, or if he's Jesus' brother or not, but he basically has a long scroll that he's rolled out and he's reading it. He says --. Let me see here. Hold on.*

Joe: *Well, let's just interview him. Let's interview this James.*

Marisa: *Okay.*

Joe: *When he's ready. Is he ready?*

Marisa: *Yeah. He says:*

(James) *"I'm ready to bring this information forth. For I am reading it directly from the scroll of life, directly from the scroll of life that was given unto me."*

Marisa: *And he keeps going. "Er-er-erm."*

Joe: *Yeah but before you read the scroll, let me ask some questions. Can I?*

Marisa: *Well, hold on. He's --.*

Joe: *Okay.*

(James) *"Reading from the scroll, the scroll of life. For I was given the task to bring this information forward into the book of life." [He's calling the Bible the Book of Life.] "I brought forth the information in which was studied, brought forth the information in which was brought to me, and I brought forth the information in which was brought to others, into something that was quite likely to be the book in which you speak of."*

Joe: So he is the author then.

Marisa: Yeah, hold on. It's kind of confusing because he is saying he's the author but what he's writing the book with, is not his information. It's like information that he's read from somewhere else.

Joe: Oh, okay. So he's probably reading some of the other writings --.

Marisa: Like, he's got a scroll --. Yeah. He has a scroll and he's reading it.

Joe: Was it from Paul? Is he reading letters from Paul?

Marisa: No. Oh, they are letters. That's what they are. The little scrolls. Yeah, they're letters.

Joe: Oh, okay.

Marisa: I feel like he's saying --.

Joe: They call them epistles. They were called epistles.

Marisa: Okay, I feel like he's saying Matthew, but I don't know if it's my mind getting into it. Hold on, let me just --. Move it, Poochie, let me lay down and focus on this guy. Now I'm getting to know the different names of the guys. I want to make sure it's not my mind getting in it. So, let's see here. Okay. All right, so he says:

(James)   *"I am James, James the first, James the first that was entered in, entered into the Bible, entered into the times, and brought forth information, brought forth information to those who remain nameless. For there are many, many who spoke, many who saw, many who gave, many who were depicted upon within these times that were no-names, that were women, that were people who brought forth information about these times in that this information was brought together into a book, so to speak. I brought this information forth, I brought this information forth indeed, and was quite revered for much of the information that was brought together. At times, people would say, 'How did you know this?' But there were people that would bring this information to me, and I would read upon it."*

Marisa: What was the book of James about?

Joe: I don't remember. It was very short. I should probably look at it again. It's a lot of rules if I remember.

Marisa: Yeah, look it up.

Joe: You want to pause that for a second?

Marisa: Yeah.

Joe: I think it's only a few pages long.

Marisa: He's basically saying --. I think your Bible is in the --. Oh, you have a Bible there?

Joe: I've got the Bible on my phone.

Marisa: Well, before you read anything out loud to me, let me just --.

Joe: I won't read it out loud.

Marisa: Yeah, he's basically saying that -- he wasn't a ghost writer --.

Joe: Don't – don't. Is that still recording?

Marisa: Yeah.

Joe: He was a ghost writer?

Marisa: Not a ghost writer, but, you know, like say, you write Baby Boomer Peace, or whatever, but Baby Boomer Peace is based off of other people's writings that you read, and you took them all, and you wrote them into something that sounded really good. So it's still your writing, but it was based off of other people's experiences.

Joe: Oh, okay. Wait a minute. This is --.

Marisa: But this is not Jesus' brother that we're talking to.

Joe: This James? It's not Jesus' brother? But is he the author of the book of James?

Marisa: Yeah.

Joe: Oh. All this time I was thinking that the author --. Now I do need to read this. Okay, this just has the Old Testament. The Holy Bible NIV. Mark --.

Marisa: Let me hit pause so this doesn't get --.

Joe: Yeah, pause that.

Marisa: That's not Jesus' brother. Okay, he's talking again. He's saying --.

Joe: Okay, he's kind of covering -- what he's doing is, he's kind of preaching on maybe the Ten Commandments --.

Marisa: Don't tell me anything yet, because he's talking. He's basically --. He's very like, "Er-er-erm." He reminds me of [inaudible*].

Joe: Is he--? Let me ask a question. Is he James, the brother of John then? If he's not the brother of Jesus, is he the brother of John, the author of the book of Revelation? Is he the brother of John, the author of the books of John and Revelation?

Marisa: He's saying no.

Joe: Was he just one of the apostles, whose name was James?

Marisa: No.

Joe: Oh, he wasn't an apostle?

Marisa: Just an author. He's a writer. He says

(James) "I am a diplomat of sorts."

Joe: Did he know Luke? Is he kind of similar to Luke?

Marisa: Let's see. Which one was Matthew?

Joe: Oh, Matthew? He was with Matthew?

Marisa: Who was Matthew?

Joe: He was the first one. Matthew was the tax collector.

Marisa: The tax collector. He feels wealthy. He feels --. He's basically coming in, having a hard time channeling because he's talking so much. He's not talking to us. He's just "blub." He just likes to talk.

Joe: Oh, well tell him to slow down and talk to us.

Marisa: He says, it's like almost like he--. Not preaching--.

Joe: Yeah, his book is preachy.

Marisa: Yeah, he's just like "blah blah blah" and "this and *this and this." And he's got this long scroll. He speaks to the wealthy. He says that he's quite --. Let's see. So this is James. James, are you the one that wrote --? He says, "Yes, I wrote this book." He says that --. Okay, stop preaching, please. He's still talking. He's reading off his little scroll. Can somebody help me, like, talk to him? Get him to stop? Hold on, Jesus is coming in but here, this James says:*

(James)   "Yes, I have brought forth the information in which would help one to see the light, see Christ, see the Word, and see the passion which lies within. For, I would like to think of myself as a poet. I would like to think of myself as an architect of words, so to speak. I would like to think of myself as someone who can eloquently bring forth truth that is held in the light of God. Many who studied the words in which were written about the Christ were able to understand and see --."

Marisa: Hold on. Now I told him to slow down too much and now he's going too slow. Okay, come here, James. C'mon, c'mon, c'mon. Okay.

(James)   "Some people could relate and some people could not relate to a story that they were told, for these stories had been told over the years, time and time and time again, that there would be a savior, that there would be a savior indeed. For, when one could look at the story and say, 'I do not believe this,' they could still look at teachings, teachings, and say, 'This is something that I can relate to'. In the Bible in the Jewish teachings, there was much destruction, there was much death, there was much wars, there was much wrath coming from the hand of God, and understanding and knowing that whether the Messiah had come or not, people needed to live appropriately. People needed to live with God inside of them. People needed to live knowing that, when looking upon another, they were looking upon themselves, looking upon God. Regardless of what human beings do, regardless of what spirit does while in the human being to prove that spirit exists, I had an inner desire to share

the appropriateness of human behavior unto each other, bringing forth the light of God through the teachings, through the ministering of what I saw was to be appropriate, through the writings and teachings that I had studied."

Marisa: So, he looks like he read a lot.   He looks like he studied a lot. He looks wealthy, very wealthy.

Joe: Well, then let me start asking him questions.

Marisa: Okay.

Joe: Ask him if it's okay if I ask questions.

Marisa: Yeah.

Joe: Okay, starting at the beginning. I don't know if I can come right out and say, where were you born? What part of the world were you born in?

Marisa: He was raised in --. I feel like he just said Jerusalem.

Joe: Okay, that's possible. Mother and father? What were they like?

Marisa: Wait. Is this the half-brother of Jesus?

Joe: That's what I'm trying to find out. I'm trying to find out whether --.

Marisa: I thought he just said Mary and James.

Joe: Well, Jesus' dad's name was Joseph.

Marisa: But if he was the half-brother --.

Joe: Well, Jesus' brothers and sisters are all half-brothers and sisters, because Joseph was not the seed for Jesus. But Mary was the womb.

Marisa: Oh, I get it. So Mary wasn't with anyone else before.

Joe: No, Mary had the Immaculate Conception.

Marisa: Yeah. Okay hold on. I feel like he said Mary and James were. The mother and father were Mary and James.

Joe: Well, let's ask him again. Are you the half-brother then of Jesus? Did you come from the same parents as Jesus?

Marisa: No.

Joe: Okay. And your mother and father's names were Mary and James? What were your mother and father's names?

Marisa: Let me see.

Joe: He's probably saying it doesn't matter.

Marisa: Pretty much. But he's saying it's nobody that anybody would ever know.

Joe: Okay, so it's not important. Brothers and sisters?

Marisa: Seven brothers and sisters.

Joe: Where did he fit in? Was he first, second, third, middle, youngest?

Marisa: He was the fourth and --.

Joe: Middle child?

Marisa: Yeah. Fourth, middle child. He's basically just saying that his childhood really isn't --.

Joe: Isn't important.

Marisa: He's saying it isn't important. What's important is *when --.*

Joe: Okay then let me ask a question. If the upbringing in his life was nothing really dramatic, in his youth as he was growing up, was he a follower in the physical of Jesus? Since he was not an apostle what was your relationship with Jesus? Was it after Jesus had been resurrected, died on the cross and resurrected? Or, did you know Jesus before he was put on the cross?

Marisa: What the heck? He just disappeared. Get back here. Poof. He disappeared. Where'd he go? Hold on.

Joe: Maybe he's irritated with me.

Marisa: No, he's not irritated. He's coming back with somebody.

Joe: Really?

Marisa: He says, "Is this who you want to talk to?"

Joe: Who's with him?

Marisa: He has Jesus' brother James.

Joe: Oh, yeah. Let's talk to both of them.

Marisa: He says, "Is this who you want to talk to?" He says, "If you want to talk to a writer, I'm the writer."

Joe: Then I want to talk to him and I want to talk to Jesus' brother.

Marisa: He says that he was just a writer.

Joe: Okay, if he was a writer, was he – did he meet Jesus? Like, Luke never met Jesus.

Marisa: He says, no, he did not meet Jesus. He says he met a *lot of the wealthy, diplomatic people and he was wealthy, but he wrote, he wrote and --. He's very unclear about the whole thing. It's almost like he's like a combination of a bunch of people, like a bunch of people wrote stuff, and the church stuck it all together and said, "Here, write all this down." Hold on. Let me ask him if his name is James. Ah! His name isn't James.*

Joe: Really? But—why? Did the church put his name --?

Marisa: This is the person that wrote the book of James, but we're not talking to James.

Joe: Oh he wrote --? The person we're talking to's name is not James?

Marisa: He's a church diplomat.

Joe: So was the author of the book of James --?

Marisa: His name was not James. Okay I get it. Okay, I was so confused.

Joe: Yeah, explain it.

Marisa: Okay, so he is a--.

Joe: Like a scribe, or something?

Marisa: No, he's not a scribe. The person that --. Because we called in, literally called in the author of James. We didn't call in James. We said we want to call in the author of James.

Joe: Oh!

Marisa: So this guy came in and he's wearing like church robes, the black robes, like a judge almost, like a diplomat, and it looks like he took a lot of the books the apostles wrote, and he turned them into something. He said that it needed to be --. He says he went and worked for the church because he grew up with a deeper understanding inside of him that goodness in people existed, and that he knew how to write, he wanted to write, but he feels like the church kind of told him, well, take all these and turn them into something.

Joe: Why did they call it the book of James?

Marisa: He says that--. Hold on, because now James the brother of Jesus is here and there's another James over here. It's like we're calling in every James on the planet.

Joe: Yeah, okay, yeah, I know that was a very common name.

Marisa: Yeah, so anyways, so, let's see. So, author of James, can you tell us why it's called James?

(James) "Much to the belief of many, James was that which was like you just said, a common name. James was that which was a name that meant one that would be just, one that would give their life, one that would be a man of God. Therefore, much that was written about in this book was being a man of God."

Marisa: There's no way I could have known that.

Joe: No way, huh-uh.

Marisa: No way.

Joe: No.

Marisa: James the brother is next to him and he is saying that the book was not written by him.

Joe: Oh, okay.

Marisa: But that the book was inspired by him.

Joe: The book of James was inspired by the brother of Jesus?

Marisa: Yes, yes.

Joe: But the brother of Jesus did not write it?

Marisa: So I have a question really quick, just so I can clarify this in my own mind. Was it you who said that people called Jesus' brother James the Just, or –

Joe: I did, but only recently, not when we were doing this.

Marisa: No, I know. But what I'm thinking is – when I say, "Who's James the Just?" I feel like James the Just is somebody completely different than Jesus' brother. That's why I feel like there's two James.

Joe: Well, everybody in church calls Jesus' brother, James the Just.

Marisa: Oh, really? So James the Just –

Joe: He was sort of like a – when people wanted to go get wisdom, so to speak, they would go find James.

Marisa: Oh, okay.

Joe: After Jesus had died.

Marisa: Let me see. So I'm calling in James the Just. Okay there's "Er-er-erm."

Joe: He's probably like a judge.

Marisa: Well, that's who I'm hearing, that "er-er-er-erm."

That is James the Just, but James the brother is not the same person.

Joe: Well, let's keep going. Let's figure this out.

Marisa: Okay. Again, remember, you're going to be in the end writing this book so –

Joe: I know.

Marisa: – we need to understand if –

Joe: I'll figure it all out.

Marisa: Yeah. You need to map it out.

Marisa: Did not write it. No.

Joe: It was inspiration...?

Marisa: Let me see. God, how many James are going to be in here? We need to be specific. Jesus, could you come help, please?

Joe: Yeah, let's see if we can get Jesus to fill in some gaps here. Because I do want to talk to his brother, because I want to get his take on Jesus. But let's ask Jesus to kind of fix this so we understand it better.

Marisa: Okay, here's Jesus. He says:

(Jesus) "Many of the books of the Bible were not written even by the apostles in which many believe wrote them. They were stories or accounts of these people, stories and accounts of my brethren, they were stories inspired by these people. It would be as if the two of you wrote an account of your life for this year of 2015 and then somebody came along, taking your personal*

journaling's that you have written throughout this entire year, every single day, and were to take a summary of these and turn them into a story, turn them into something that was understandable, and then take the stories that were written about the personal rantings, at times, that the two of you wrote each day, on your own, and turn them into a book, take them to a church and have the church say, 'We must have one of our grandest writers take these stories and turn them into something inspirational'. So, yes, my brother James was somebody who was mentioned in the Bible, but not many times at all. Much of my family was not mentioned. For it appeared in the Bible that I was more of a lone warrior to make me seem less human, less as if I had close friends, less as if I had brothers and sisters, less as if I was a child where I was just born and then I was an adult and I was God. So understand the way that many of these books were written were to bring highlights to the people that surrounded me that were known to have surrounded me, to understand so that people could read upon these pages and gain inspiration from them, but also gain the need to follow God's word, but also have the faith and knowing that a messiah had come to the world, a messiah that so many had been waiting for had come to save them. This was to bring inspiration and faith to the world."

Marisa: James, the brother, didn't write any books and it doesn't seem like he was mentioned very much in the Bible. This other guy, he's just a hired writer.

Joe: It just seems to me that I've read in the --. You know, when you open up the Bible, there in the margins, it has stories, theologians have written stories, historians, theological historians, I believe, have said that the book of James is from the brother of Jesus. But I'm going to have to go back and check that. But I'm going to go with what we're doing here. Does it make any sense, Jesus, to talk to your brother right now, or is it just something --? Would it be the same as talking to one of your sisters or your next door neighbor, or something? Is it *instrumental to our book to be interviewing your brother James? I mean, I'd like to. I'd like to get his --.*

Marisa: It's funny. He says, "If you would like to, if you would like to."

Joe: Okay, I'd like to. I'd like to ask him a few questions.

Marisa: Okay.

Joe: Is he here?

Marisa: Yeah.

Joe: Is he willing to talk?

Marisa: Yeah. He's actually coming in kind of like a kid. He's coming in young.

Joe: Then ask the brother of Jesus -- James-- if he's got any opening words, then I'll ask him some specific questions. Does he have anything that he'd like to say first?

Marisa: Okay, this is the brother of Jesus and he says...

(Brother James) "No, sir. I will let you ask unto me what you would like to ask unto me."

Joe: He does sound like a young man when referring to me as a sir.

Marisa: He's about 15.

Joe: Oh, okay. I'm going to guess then, James, were you about 15 when Jesus left the home and went on his journeys? How old were you when your brother Jesus --Yeshua, I'm sure you called him Yeshua -- about how old were you when Yeshua left the home in your hands?

(Brother James) *"He was important, oh yes, they would say that he was going to bring the light on this day and bring it unto us, so that we may see that the world would be bringing into our sight something quite miraculous, something quite fabulous, something quite extraordinary, for we didn't get to see how great they say he became."*

Marisa: Did he die young? He says he was about 12 when Jesus left.

Joe: How old was Jesus at the time when he left?

Marisa: It looks like about 17 or 18.

Joe: Okay, all right. That's a big gap. Is this James, Jesus' brother, is he the oldest brother of Jesus? Not the oldest brother, but the eldest, the one --.

Marisa: The youngest?

Joe: Not the youngest. The one that comes right after him.

Marisa: No.

Joe: Really?

Marisa: It looks like it's --. Okay I see Jesus and then I see two, and then I see James.

Joe: Were the two both boys, or were they boy and girl, or girls?

Marisa: I can't tell. I can't tell, I just see--. The way they're showing me is kind of like a light where Jesus is, and then they show "doot doot," two little markings, and then they show James.

Joe: So you were 12 and Jesus is about 18, and so –

Marisa: I think there were two James. Jesus, did you have two brother's named James? He says yes. Can I channel about this, or is my mind going to get stuck in the way? He says,

(Jesus) "Oh, my dear brother and sister, what you must understand is that the language in which your books are written in is not the language in which we wrote them in, and the names in which we went by are not the names in which you have within this book. The names that we went by were very different indeed for many of us went by the house we were from, the town we were from, and the name in which we bore with the name of the qualities that we carried. So many times there would be several of the same name in the same family. This was due to the characteristics, but –"

Marisa: Were they like nicknames? He says, "No nicknames." So were they both named James when they were born? "No." So they got named James later. "Yes." Why were they named James?" One James died." Oh, one James is named after the other James? "No." Gosh, this is so confusing.

Joe: Let's keep reading then. Maybe we'll learn more.

Marisa: We might, but let me just see. Okay. And so is that James the Just over there? And he goes, "Er-er-er-erm. That's me." Okay. Are you an actual person, or are you just an energy field? He says, "I'm an energy field." Oh, okay. So you're not an actual person….He's an energy field. Okay, but this is an actual person over here. This is the eight-year-old James that saw his brother heal a lamb in the shed, and he was younger than Jesus. Where's the older James, the James that was older than him? Okay, Jesus' older brother James is on another planet. He's like way over there.

Joe: Okay, can we call him in?

Marisa: Okay, now we have the older brother of Jesus in here.

Joe: But that is – I don't think I'm going to put it in the book, because again Jesus doesn't want me to add to or detract from anything from the Bible, and if I was to put in there that Jesus had an older brother named James, I mean, it would just blow the whole New Testament out of the water.

Marisa: Yeah.

Joe: It would just –

Marisa: Oh, not an older brother, I mean like there's the older one and the younger one.

Joe: Oh, an older James and a younger James?

Marisa: Yeah. Wait, let me see.

Joe: Well, according to the Bible, James is the Number 2 child. He was the first child following Jesus, well actually, Yeshua –

Marisa: Yeah, that's what I'm seeing so –

Joe: And then you're saying there's a younger James also?

Marisa: There's a younger James, like three down. Let me see.

Joe: How many are in between the James?

Marisa: There's three in between each James.

Joe: So there's James like the first, and then James the second, or something.

Marisa: James the Just, are you an actual person? He feels like he's more just like a... This is so confusing. There is an older child though, older than Jesus though. They just won't show it to me. It's like a sparkling...

Joe: **Yeah. There's no way I'm going to put that in there.**

Marisa: Yeah, I know. I don't expect you to. Unless I fully understood it or was like completely... unless I was completely in trance asking about it, I wouldn't trust my mind.

Joe: Yipes!

Marisa: I know, exactly. Okay. Well, keep reading, and then – I'm just trying to figure out this puzzle of all these James everywhere.

Joe: Some of this will come together.

Marisa: Yeah.

Marisa: And he's very innocent looking. He looks like he plays with sheep all day.

Joe: Oh really?

Marisa: Yeah, he's like very innocent and sweet and nice, and I'm not quite sure why he's coming in as a 12-year-old. I guess that's maybe the last time he knew Jesus. No? Uh-uh. He grew up and he met up with him. Why are you coming in as a 12-year-old, James? Okay, hold on, here comes James' higher self.

Joe: Is it because he felt inferior to Jesus?

Marisa: No. He says --.

Joe: Did he look up to him?

Marisa: *He says they knew you were going to ask of the childhood, so they wanted to bring the childhood self.*

Joe: *Oh, okay.*

Marisa: *So they said he was anticipating your questions so he was appearing as a 12-year-old to talk about their simple roots, their simple lives, their simple nature, and their understanding that the morning star, or the morning light --. He's talking about something. Hold on, let me talk to the higher self. It's easier. Okay, hold on. Samuel, can you help me connect with these guys? I'm having a hard time.*

Joe: *I guess in his youth I was just going to ask him what was it like. Was there anything extraordinary? Was Jesus extraordinary, or was he like a typical big brother?*

(Brother James) "I love my brother. I love my brother. He was kind and gentle and nice. He never hit me. He never teased me. We laughed and we played. My parents treated him a little bit differently. They didn't let him play as much as we do, but our life was not an easy one growing up. We worked hard."

Marisa: *They're showing him growing up. They're showing him meeting Jesus and they're showing him watching Jesus getting killed.*

Joe: *Oh man. Did he participate in any of the ministry?*

Marisa: *Yeah, he's showing that it was almost like a delayed --. He loved his brother and he believed in his brother, but it's not that he necessarily was like "oh my brother is god" by any means. It was more like, I think, after everything happened, he kind of went out and started preaching the Word.*

Joe: *So to him --.*

Marisa: *He was just his brother.*

Marisa P. Moris and Joseph P. Moris

Joe: He was just a brother.

Marisa: Yeah, he says,

(Brother James) "Yes, it's Yeshua. It's my brother." He's a nice guy. He's sweet. He doesn't pick on me. He doesn't beat me up. And we play with the sheep together. And you know, it was just a very innocent ---

Marisa: He's very innocent, very nice, very sweet, very just. You know, he's just very –.

Joe: Okay, let me ask him a question. Okay, James, how old were you when you had your first girlfriend?

Marisa: He just blushed.

Joe: Okay, fine. How old was he when he fell in love for the first time?

Marisa: He says 17.

Joe: Oh, really? That late? I would have expected maybe a little younger than that. Did he ever see Jesus have a crush on a girl?

Marisa: No.

Joe: Okay. So he was godly from the get-go?

Marisa: Mm-hm.

Joe: Hm. That's interesting.

Marisa: He says no. He says,

(Brother James) "My brother was the best example"

Marisa: He idolizes him. You can tell. He thinks he's the

coolest person in the world—

(Brother James) "He was the best example and he was very patient and very kind and he loved me so much, even when my dad would get mad."

Marisa: He says, one time it started raining and it rained so hard that the roof started to fall in, in one of the farms -- looks like they had little sheds, kind of -- and he says that one of the animals was giving birth, like a lamb or something, and it was raining real hard and the roof was falling in, and he says that his brother went out and helped the animal give birth, like healing it. Yeah. He says that the --.

Joe: Oh, the animal was having trouble and maybe it was going to die in childbirth, or something?

Marisa: Yeah, yeah. Like the animal, he's showing the animal, it's like a mule or a sheep or something --.

Joe: Having trouble delivering.

Marisa: --It was giving birth, and it was raining real hard and the roof was falling in, and the animal was, like, scared. And he says that he looked outside and he says he saw balls of light in his hands.

Joe: In Jesus' hands?

Marisa: Yeah. And he was helping it heal.

Joe: About how old was Jesus at that time?

Marisa: About 17.

Joe: So it was just shortly before he left?

Marisa: Yeah, but he didn't know that anybody could see him. He wasn't doing it so anyone could see him. But he says, he saw it. And he never said anything.

Joe: Jesus didn't talk about it?

Marisa: Yeah, like Jesus didn't say "Oh, look what I can do," and he never talked about it. He just went out there and he helped the animal. And James says he saw it, but he didn't tell anybody.

Joe: Oh, so he understood his brother better – when?– after Jesus was crucified? Or before he was crucified?

Marisa: He says he saw him do that, and just thought he couldn't believe his eyes. He just thought maybe it was the lightning, or the weather was weird. It was raining and the roof was falling in and he saw light coming from there.

Joe: From his hands?

Marisa: Yeah. So after everything happened, and after he started hearing the stories of the healings and all this stuff, he thought of that, and that's when he believed it. But he didn't believe it (when Jesus lived at home). Even though they talked about it when he was young, like, "Oh, the angels came and said he was going to come and be born," and all that stuff, it was still like, "Oh he's just my brother," and when he saw that, he still thought he was just seeing things. But then when he started -- when everybody started talking about Jesus healing people, he thought back to that, and went, "Oh, that's what he was doing," and then he believed it.

Joe: Oh, that's interesting. We'll certainly talk to Jesus about his mom and dad, and what happened to his dad, and everything else (in the next book called Ask Jesus). So, I'm going to save that question. I don't want to ask James specifics on Joseph and Mary. Except Mary. I'd like to get his (Brother James') take on his mom. Who was the authoritarian in the family? Was it Mary, his mother Mary? Or his dad, Joseph?

(Brother James)It was dad.

Joe: Your dad Joseph was the --? Like the disciplinarian?

(Brother James)Yes.

Joe: So, his mom was sweet. But did she ever lose her temper or anything?

(Brother James)No, she was sharp.

Marisa: He's showing her as --- seeing her up close. It's scary looking showing her with a thing over her head, kind of like you see in the pictures, I think. And they're showing her extremely heavy, like fat.... very overweight. Or is she pregnant?

Joe: Is that because she's pregnant or something?

Marisa: Maybe she's pregnant.

Joe: Probably always having babies. How many brothers and sisters?

Marisa: Seven.

Joe: Seven brothers and sisters.

Marisa: So, yeah, she looks heavy. Her face looks very round, but the way that I see Mary, you know, pictures, they show this sweet, young, little 14-year-old girl. But they're showing a woman with dark brown hair. She looks very Israeli. She looks very --. Not Israeli. Middle Eastern.

Joe: I was going to say. Israelites would have like --this is a generalization--having larger noses.

Marisa: Well, she kind of --- she has dark hair, kind of bad teeth.

Marisa P. Moris and Joseph P. Moris

Joe: They didn't have dentists in those days.

Marisa: And her eyes are very deep-set. And she does, she kind of has a nose like this. Kind of like the arch. Like a rounded nose.

Joe: That's kind of in the Jewish vein.

Marisa: Yeah, Jewish. Right.

Joe: They were all Jews.

Marisa: Yeah, okay, so yeah. She looks like a Jewish woman. That's what she looks like. She looks (like) an East Coast Jewish woman. But you know, not very good teeth. But her hair, she has bangs, kind of. Or dark hair kind of swept over to the side. Kind of like this. And she's got salt and pepper. So, it's like she's older. He's showing her-- oh, he's showing her before she died. And they're making a stew or something like that. She's making stew.

Joe: Okay. She had seven kids --.

Marisa: Yeah, the kids are all sitting around, and he's basically just showing her like a regular old mom, like cooking food. Its lamb they're eating, or something like that.

Joe: So he generally went off and lived his own life, and apart from Jesus' teachings. Eventually, did he get married, have children, etcetera?

Marisa: Married, two children. He says he didn't have a very magnificent life, the type of life that someone would expect from a brother of Jesus...you know, someone who became well known ---

Joe: Fame....

Marisa: Yeah. But --.

Joe: So, basically, he had a nondescript life. He had a wife, he had kids. He went out and worked every day to provide for his family.

Marisa: Yeah. He just had a normal life.

Joe: Nothing, nothing fabulous. He didn't start a church and start a ministry or anything like that?

Marisa: He taught the kids, and he believed in miracles. And it feels like he kind of ran with them for a little bit, like he was part of the crew for a little bit, like it feels like I see him with Peter and stuff.

Joe: Okay, so he became a Christian. He didn't stay a Jew?

Marisa: Yeah. No, it feels like he ran with their crew a little bit. I see him kind of like --. Here comes Peter with his little hat. But it feels like he knew them. James, did you stay Jewish? Feels like he did stay Jewish. Hold on a second. They didn't call it Christian right after Jesus died. Did they?

Joe: No.

Marisa: That's what he said. They didn't call it--he said --.

Joe: They were all Jews. But the Gentiles were starting to come in. The Gentiles were the non-Jews.

Marisa: Okay, yeah. Because he just said, he says, "There's no such thing as Christian." We're talking to the "him" back then. He's going, "What's Christian?"

Joe: Yeah, all right. That makes sense. How old was he when he passed away?

Marisa: 56.

Joe: So, yeah. The churches and everything, didn't really start *popping up until the Christian faith itself all started happening, maybe in the 200s to the 300s AD.*

Marisa: Jesus said "236."

Joe: 236? That's like an official year when Christianity was recognized--?

Marisa: Jesus says--.

Joe: --as a faith?

Marisa: Yeah. Well, he just, when we said Christianity, he said, 236, is what he said.

Joe: Well I want to fit James into this book on the authors.

Marisa: I'm curious --.

Joe: It's nice to get a different story.

Marisa: I like the story about the sheep.

Joe: I think it's a great story. Jesus, is that real? Is Jesus still here?

Marisa: Yeah, yeah. He says --.

Joe: Jesus, did that happen? Did you keep the roof from falling in, too? James says that you went out and healed an animal who was giving birth, and the roof was falling in, and that was disturbing the animal, whether it was a sheep or it probably --.

Marisa: He says,

(Jesus) "Yes, I went outside when the hail storm came and it started to cause the structure of the small steeple that we *had built for the lamb that was going to give birth."* It was like a small tent that was built for the delivering lambs.

Marisa: You know, with like – he's showing me – like straw over – like they took wood, you know, like this, and they put straw. But it was a little thing so that the --.

Joe: Oh, it was like a palapa?

Marisa: Yeah. They made like a little house for it so that it could lay under there and be safe and give birth.

Joe: From the rain.

Marisa: Yeah, and it wasn't even for the rain. It's like they made it feel safe, or something. It's like they loved the animals just as much --. They said animals--. Like people would slay the animals to eat them or whatever, but it's like he loved all the animals. He would talk to them. He says:

(Jesus)   "I would speak to the animals because I saw their spirit inside."

Joe: Like Marisa does.

Marisa: And he felt the spirit inside and he would see the beauty of the father and the mother coming from within the animal in giving birth into a creation that had breath. He says,

(Jesus)   "When you see the breath rise and fall, even from a mule, you understand and see that each breath is sacred, each breath brings wisdom and each breath brings knowledge. And although an animal may not have the capacity to speak unto the humans, they surely have the divinity of God within them, for they blink, for they sniff, they smell, for they walk about the earth just as humans walk about the earth, and they think and they sense, just as humans think and sense. But human beings many times believe that they own the earth, when in fact the earth

owns the human beings. For when we bring about the beauty of God within each living creature, and we see God in each living creature, it makes us realize that we are just a creation, just like the animal. So I would look upon them, look into their eyes, and I could feel them and sense them. So, yes, my brother saw when one evening I began to feel a surging in my hands at times. I began to feel a surge within my lower belly at times. I began to feel a surging within my feet, and within my temples. And these were energies that I felt, as if I had to place upon others, or place upon something. So when my hands began to surge, I knew that something needed me to place them upon them. So when the hailstorm came, and the small structure in which we had created for Agah, the name of the lamb, I ran out and I placed my hands upon her, as she was afraid that she would die, she was afraid that she would be smashed upon by the home and was afraid to give birth to her child. So I placed my hands upon Agah and brought forth the life in which she was delivering. I did not think that anybody saw me. But it is apparent now, and of course I know now, that my dear brother saw this and witnessed this. Many a times this happened, especially when in the ministry, in starting the ministry, as my hands would begin to feel the surge, the surge of the heat entering into them, whereby knowing that this needed to be transferred unto somebody else. This was one of the first times I felt this, so much so that I felt and saw light outside of myself."

Joe: That was the first time he realized his healing powers?

Marisa: It was actually the third time, the third time. "But it was the first time where" –. He's showing it's the first time where he actually went "whoa."

Joe: "This is cool."

Marisa: Yeah.

Joe: Okay. But he wasn't egotistical. He didn't run around going, "Hey, look what I can do."

Marisa: No. He says he began to play with the energies. He began to form energy between his hands, move it along different parts of his body. He's saying that he would feel the different energies and he would soon deliver this account to schools that taught this healing energy. Once his parents knew of it, he was sent to mystery schools, or something like that, where they knew how to work with energy, or something.

Joe: Really?

Marisa: Yeah.

Joe: Wow. About what age was he when he first went off to those --?

Marisa: 17.

Joe: 17. So technically that's when he left his home?

Marisa: Yes.

Joe: And who was put in charge as the oldest child? Well, you know what? Let's not go there. Those are all the things I'm going to ask when I get to interview you, Jesus, for the Ask Jesus book. Let's go back to James. Let's go back to both James's. Well, actually the author, the writer, was not named James.

Marisa: No. Uh-uh.

Joe: Do either one of them have any closing statements before we wrap up this chapter?

Marisa: Okay, so the older version of James, James' higher self or whatever, is a pretty good looking, strapping guy. Looks like --. I want to say Roman. Not Roman. He's got like a--. He's wearing a short sleeve, like brown, like V-neck type shirt. You know, made out of --. Not burlap or whatever. And he's got a knapsack across his chest, like he carried books in it, or *something. Not books, but --. You know, kind of a backpack type thing he's got across his chest.*

Joe: This is James the brother, or the author?

Marisa: Yeah, James the brother. James the brother.

Joe: Not the writer.

Marisa: Grown up. And he looks like --. Let me see what he has to say.

Joe: So he didn't gain a great deal of popularity? In other words, he didn't become like a rock star because he was the brother of Jesus. He just lived a normal life.

Marisa: No, he died before Jesus got real popular. Like he's saying people didn't believe, or they believed. And the people that did believe weren't really people that were around where he was. It was like, it's hard to explain. He's hard to talk to. It's like --. I keep getting the kid.

Joe: Probably because he wasn't involved in Jesus' ministry.

Marisa: Yeah, probably not. They probably are just bringing what --.

Joe: What he remembers and --.

Marisa: Yeah.

Joe: You know, six years or seven years, five, six, seven years is a big gap between the ages of brothers and sisters, especially when the older one leaves home. That was pretty similar to my own brothers Randy and Steve. They didn't really know my brother Mike and I very well. Because we were older and we left home when we were 17, and Randy and Steve were like 12 and 13. Other than seeing us at dinner or whatever, they didn't really know much about Mike and I until long after we had all grown up and got to know each other. So anyway, okay. Anybody else in this little circle being Jesus--?

Marisa: *He says the one that wrote it --.*

Joe: *Does he have anything to say?*

Marisa: *The author James, he's just basically looks like, he kind of looks like what Peter's higher self looks like. He looks like a Lutheran church leader, or something like that.*

Joe: *Oh, those funny looking black caps?*

Marisa: *Yeah. Well, now, it's almost like he has a wig on, with you know--. No, not like a Jewish cap. He just --. The one that came in, the author of James, he has that scroll or whatever.*

Joe: *Well, ask him if he's got any parting words, and then he'll now be famous because --.*

Marisa: *Well, no, he's saying that he helped found a church.*

Joe: *What's his name?*

Marisa: *I think its James. I'm so confused.*

Joe: *I thought he said earlier that his name was not James. He was the author of the book of James.*

Marisa: *He's the author of James. It's very, very confusing. I don't know. I don't know if I said it was James, I would just be guessing.*

Joe: *Well, maybe we shouldn't have that part in the book.*

Marisa: *This is what I see. What I'm seeing without channeling is, I'm seeing a man with a big cross on his chest, a big gold cross on his chest, with black robes, long, flowing robes, and he's got a long scroll, and he's reading everyone else's stories and their accounts, and kind of bringing them together into, almost like a poetic justice --. Yeah, like a teacher. And I feel like his name is James, but I don't think that he's the brother, because I see the brother as a 12-year-old kid, and I see the higher self of the kid as just a simple, you know, everyday guy.*

Joe: Everyday man.

Marisa: Looks like he knows how to read and write, because he's carrying around books and something to write on.

Joe: Like an average, middle-class person?

Marisa: Yeah. But there's so many --. It seems like there's a lot of --. Between these three that I'm seeing, it seems like there's a lot of, like, discrepancies in what people believe. And I think that's why I'm having a hard time depicting it. Like, Rosemary is saying,

(Rosemary) "Everybody thinks that Jesus' brother wrote the book. A lot of people think that but everybody thinks something different but Jesus' brother was a very sweet person, a nice person.

Marisa: Yeah, I do not think he wrote the book.

Joe: I can picture that group of Constantine saying that, look, this gives legitimacy. Let's put the name of Jesus' brother, James, on this one.

Marisa: Yeah.

Joe: And it was a fabrication of the council of Constantine and they gave credit to Jesus' brother to give it legitimacy but now we're finding out what the truth is.

Marisa: Oh, okay. Because I don't want to be getting it

wrong, but I mean, I see what I see. And it just doesn't --.

Joe: Well, he's already told us, all these authors have told us what the council did...how they operated for Constantine and his council, even though they had come to love Jesus still had their biases....

Marisa: Oh, I don't remember what they said.

Joe: .... and they also needed a book that would basically be a best seller. You know what I mean? But we're not going to criticize the Bible, because it is the best possible depiction of man's relationship with God. So even if there is some faultiness in areas, that's not our concern at this point.

Marisa: Yeah.

Joe: Okay, so let's put a period on that. Thank you, Mr. Author.... James.... not author but writer of the manuscript of James. And thank you, James, the brother of Jesus.

Marisa: He's really sweet. I like him.

Joe: The kid?

Marisa: Yeah.

James Clarification

6-17-2016

Marisa: We have questions about James. So James, what I want to figure out is ... well, Jesus, now that you're here and your energy is so strong ...

Joe: Well, in here it mentioned that one James died even before Jesus died. One James died even before Jesus, but in the Bible, after Jesus is executed that the apostles are told, or the apostles tell people that they need to go talk to the brother of Jesus who is 'James the Just' but they don't go into any details. So, who is James the Just? Is that the brother that just – is this something I should be asking now or wait until tomorrow? Who is James the Just?

Marisa: We can ask now. He says....and he's laughing. He says, "There're three James the Just if you really look at it."

Joe: Who was the Bible referring to when they say, "James the Just," because they –

Marisa: James the Just is a man –

Joe: But they're saying it's your brother. Are they speaking of your brother?

(Jesus) "No.... the word, 'brother' is thrown around a lot...brother, sister, brethren...so in translation, many times apostles or even cousins or close friends were called upon as brothers, sisters, family. It's a term that they used. 'James the Just' is just a character made up in the Bible."

Joe: Oh, great. Ay yay yay. I can't go there...!

(Jesus) "James the Just is – let me put it this way; as time passes by, as the years went by, people told stories by the fire, people told stories around their – around their homes. Many began to give names, give nicknames – for lack of a better word – to the different personalities of our time. For if you were to call in all of the names that are used to describe people, you would get maybe six to ten different energies coming in. This is why this is a little complicated for us because this channel can see so many dimensions. If she could just see one or two dimensions, then it would not be so confusing, but what she is actually seeing is the morphic fields of made-up characters. She's seeing the spirits, she's seeing the higher selves, she's seeing all the different energies of all the different phases of their life. So what we suggest to you, what we suggest to you is to remind her that when we do this channeling tomorrow to call in the actual human that was my brother, the human being that was my brother that was named James at birth. When you speak unto him you will find that this is the brother that saw me with the lamb.

Joe: Did he die before you died?

(Jesus) "No, he did not."

Marisa P. Moris and Joseph P. Moris

Joe: Okay. Something in our tapings here said that he died – he died before you died.

Marisa: Nope, he did not, not the one with the lamb. There is another James. That James died when he was three.

Joe: Oh. I can't imagine a family naming more than one son James but then again, well, George Foreman named all seven of his sons George.

Marisa: Hahahaha. That's like that show, my brother Darryl and my other brother Darryl....

(Jesus) "James is a meaning. James is a meaning, so there would be James of this or James of that or James – James the –"

Marisa: Like he's showing me James the Happy, James the Angry, James the whatever.

Joe: Oh, okay.

(Jesus) "So many times we would go by those terms of endearment but this is not like Yeshua Ben Joseph. This is like 'Yeshua the Happy' ben Joseph. It was like Yeshua the Happy ben Joseph... of the Joseph, of this town."

Marisa: So he's showing like these long names that they would have but their name meant something, so if the baby came through and they said, "Oh, they're so 'this' then they name it that.

Joe: Aww, well then technically what we found out then is that James means 'Just'.

Marisa: Yeah, really. That's pretty crazy if it really does mean that.

Joe: It does.

Marisa: Oh, my gosh. Well, that's crazy. Okay, so anyways he's saying –

Joe: And I'm not sure where I read that, whether it's –

Marisa: He says, James the Just – well, they said that in the reading that James the Just is this guy up here who is coming in and he says, "I'm James the Just," and he's the one that called James 'James the Just' in the Bible, and he is a diplomat, a judge-looking guy. His name is James also and then he's got another guy next to him named James and a guy next to him named David and they are scribes. This guy James compiled information from Ruth, Mary, Seraphina, Sariah and some names I don't understand. He was in charge of taking all the texts from the women and turning them into men, this guy, this judge is the "Er-er-er-erm" guy.

Joe: I guess it's because nobody would pay any attention to a woman back in those days.

Marisa: Yeah. So it feels like the writings of James – it may not be a big book, but this guy that's coming in as like a judge that wrote it and put it together had a hand in 113 books in the Bible.

Joe: There aren't even that many books in the Bible.

Marisa: I don't know. That's what he's saying. Maybe all of them didn't go in.

Joe: Well, in one of our other books, Constantine was working with 222 books and he ended up with 22 books in the New Testament, and that's it.

Marisa: Yeah. So he's saying 113, but it's even showing like old testament stuff too. It's like – this guy is like the government. I think he represents –yeah, he's got this long scroll, and he's got all of the teachings and they're all piled around him. Looks like he and a whole bunch of people are in there, and they're going through them going "How about this? How about this? How about this? and he's looking at it all. He looks like a judge with the white George-Washington hair, and he's going, "Take this, take this, take this and strike that". Instead of using the women's scrolls they're saying it's Joseph not Josephine.... not Jamilah, it's James." You know, it's like they were changing the credit to men and going through everything and just kind of –

Joe: Well, that's how the Book of James, the two Book of James are anyway. There's no personality in there at all. It's all rules and – not affirmations. What's the opposite of affirmations?

Marisa: Rules, laws.

Joe: Yeah, kind of rules and laws.

Marisa: They're telling you what to do and how to live is what he's saying.

Joe: Condemnations and things like that. If you don't follow this, if you don't follow that – it's just kind of very dry and almost like a political text which is kind of odd when it supposedly comes from the brother of Jesus.

Marisa: It's not the brother of Jesus, that's why. It's not the brother of Jesus.

Joe: Then the theologians are way off. My guess is the theologians do a lot of guessing and then they put it all into their texts in the margins of the Bible. I mean there are schools of theology all over the country, all over the world that people study, but you can bet – I'm sure that every single teacher and theologian has a different idea on how to teach the Bible, so we have come to 2,000 years later where we've just gotten this real cacophony of thought, and its kind of weird. Okay, I do want to speak with Rosemary – it's quarter to 2:00, so I've got to go.

Marisa: Okay.

Joe: So back tomorrow in the morning or afternoon tomorrow?

Marisa: Morning.

James Review about Christ, Joseph and James

6-18-2016

Marisa: Okay. I'll just say a prayer even though it's clear in here. Heavenly Father God we ask that you surround this house, protect this house. We ask that you fill in these newfound vortexes – that are driving me crazy, that I can't get rid of – with Christ Light all the way down into the vortexes, into the earth only accepting and allowing beings of the highest level of love and light into them, around them, through them, into this house, into this dimension, into our world. We ask you, God, to send your angels, your personal angels to stand on all sides of this house above and below filling this house with the frequency of those angels, filling all our fields with the frequency of Gabriel; and we ask, God, that you send a gatekeeper that's for all of our highest and best good that will help me to connect the most clearly to someone that we can get this information from, so whether it's Joseph or someone that knew Joseph or someone that I can connect with very easily, as easily as I did with Einstein yesterday, I ask that you send someone in. Oh, okay, Samuel and Jesus. And we ask Jesus to fill this room with the Light of Christ protecting us from anything that's not for our highest and best good for if there are any earthbound spirits here then they can beat it. Amen. Okay. Joseph is here.

Joe: I want to talk to Jesus first about this.

Marisa P. Moris and Joseph P. Moris

Marisa: Okay. Jesus is here. Joseph is next to him. Mary is in front of him. Mary is holding a baby. He says "We are of the fifth plane of the astral plane, because we are not on this planet. This is why you see us here." Oh, they're projecting from like a different planet. Interesting. Okay. All right, open, you start.

Joe: Well, I mean it sounds like Joseph and Mary are already here, but I wanted to ask Jesus if it was okay – and first off, am I talking to the Jesus of biblical days, or am I talking to his higher self?

Marisa: Let me see the Jesus of the biblical days. Jesus' biblical days is over here. Jesus' higher self is the one we always talk to. Christ is up there.

Joe: Christ is who I'm really asking, wanting to talk to.

Marisa: You want to talk to Christ.

Joe: Since I know you're going to put zippers over your mouth if I bring up the Bible.... I want to find out if ... and I'm going to be really careful here, but the Bible states, yet we've already been told in these interviews that it's not a virgin birth but that was the philosophy of Constantine so they had to basically make up a story. Anyway, we had a lot of problems yesterday trying to figure out James' story and a lot of stuff came through. So we'd like to try to get the real story from the real father or real mother, which would be Joseph and Mary, why we are being told that there were two James. I want to know from you, Christ, if it's okay if we converse with Joseph and Mary about this subject.

(Christ) Absolutely. The truth is already in each and every one of you. The truth is already in there. It's just looking and seeing the truth and allowing the truth to come through as the truth comes through, for the beliefs and the fears and the antagonism that one has for oneself inside of oneself in a human to go against the grain is something that one may fear too much, so we give the truth. Many times you just do not hear the truth. When the channel sees zippers over mouths, sometimes this is because she does not want to hear, and sometimes it is because they do

not want to tell only because they think she or you do not want to hear, but we are an open book. We will give you any information you want. We will answer any question you want, because in universal energy, everything is the same. We are just information particles, and really the information that we give, we have no attachment to. Humans are the ones that provide attachment to certain beliefs, certain things. If one's beliefs are stricken against, one has fear that they will not be able to believe anything that they have ever believed. And then there is also the fear that they will have been wrong their entire life, or they will look stupid, or they will feel ashamed that they believed something that they thought was so clearly something that they feel they should not have believed now that they know the truth.

"So let us just say this. Let us just fill this room, let us just fill this surroundings, including the child, including the animals, with the ability to hear taken information, receive information without attachment, without attachment to what it means, without attachment to "Is this going to go in the book?" without attachment to what people say, without attachment to 'Oh, my goodness, I can't believe that I thought this, and now what are my beliefs?' Let us just fill and surround this room with the ability to listen and hear as if this is fiction and then take from it which you would like, for what we have said and what we said yesterday through one of our own is that it is not about the information. It is not about who did what, who was a virgin, who was not, who slept with who, who was married, who had a child, who did not. It is not about that at all. It is about the human condition. It is about being a human and being conflicted between spirit, body, mind; being conflicted by these things and having a spirit inside that wants to sing, that wants to play, that wants to be in joy, that wants to have fun, and a mind that says, 'You cannot do that, because that is not responsible. You cannot do that, because that is not fun. You cannot do that because that is fun.' And we say unto you, we say unto you that the earth plane is what you make the earth plane, and yes, we have said this many, many, many times before. We have said this over and over again but we cannot say it enough. We cannot say it enough that you create your own reality. You create your own reality, and you entangle your reality with others. What you choose to take on from their reality is your choice on some level. You may say,

'But my human does not know. My human does not know.' Yes, your human does not know, but your spirit does. Your higher self does. Some level of you does, so all you must do is just ask the questions. Ask the questions. *'Why am I creating this reality? What is this reality being created for?'*

"Joe, when things happen to you and you end up not being able to go and see your fiancé, you have to ask yourself this question: *'Why is big Joe doing this? What am I getting out of this? What am I getting out of it?'* This is all you must do, and as soon as you see what you are getting out of it, most cases it changes, because now you've learned your lesson. So understand that – and it is the same for all human beings – we must always ask, why is our higher self choosing this? Because unlike that which this channel believes, yes, lives are programmable and lives are charted out, but they change all the time, and we can change it all the time. We can pull in different guides; we can pull in different higher selves if we want. So we are the makers of our own destiny, and the more the world transfers into and merges into the fifth dimension, the more people will realize that they are the creators of their own destiny. You may ask any question you would like. I give you the stage."

Joe: Okay. All right. Yesterday we had a lot of confusion, and my assessment from what came from yesterday was that the most prominent James – apparently we're having three James come through. One James says nothing. One James is the young child that loves Jesus and was amazed by a miracle healing that he did on a lamb during a hailstorm. The third one is a James that said he took the compilation of all these writings that Constantine threw on his desk, and he said, "Write a book, and give it in favor of the name of the brother of Jesus, James." So apparently, the book of James wasn't even written by James, the brother of Jesus. He (Brother James) was only given the credit by another James taking let's say a thousand pages of writing and compressing it down into one small book. And then there's a third James, the one that doesn't say anything, and we've been given the idea that this James was actually the son of Joseph and had preceded Jesus, but then again we're confused. Maybe it was actually a son of Mary, but then again Mary was supposed to have been a virgin when she had Jesus, so we get these *conflicting stories. So instead of talking to the James's that we did yesterday, I want to talk to Joseph. I want to talk to the father. I want to know more about him. Nobody knows anything about Joseph other than he was called when Mary was told by Gabriel that they would have a son. And then he took Mary to Bethlehem for the census, and then we never hear from Joseph again. There's no mention of him. Nothing. So what I'd like to do is have a small conversation with Joseph, if that is okay.*

Marisa: Yeah, Jesus – Geez...Joseph has a demon on him! Christ, can we give Joseph a healing?

Joe: Make sure we've got the right Joseph. I want the Joseph who is the earthly father of Jesus ... Joseph ...

Marisa: Then I don't want to see the earthly Joseph. I want to see Joseph's higher self.

Joe: Get the higher self.

Marisa: Oh my gosh, it's Christ!

Joe: Oh, my gosh ... egads Christ was portraying himself in Joseph too. Now I'm a little confused. Apparently Christ was really spreading himself around then, wasn't he?

Marisa: Yeah.

Joe: But it was important. Was he also the higher self of Mary as well?

Marisa: No. Mary's higher self looks like she belongs to – her higher self is coming in as someone named Daphne.

Joe: Thrones. I just heard thrones (highest order of angels).

Marisa: Yeah, she's part of that too, yeah, but whoever Daphne is. Daphne, I think, is a Greek goddess. Daphne is the wife of Alpheus.

Marisa P. Moris and Joseph P. Moris

Alpheus turned Daphne into a tree.

Joe: Not to get off on a tangent --

Marisa: Hold on. I'm just looking at the higher selves. So okay, so Daphne –

Joe: I want the higher self of Joseph.

Marisa: Okay. The higher self of Joseph . . . Yeah, Mary is an angel and so is Joseph. They're both angelic beings. Okay, so Joseph's higher self?

Joe: Yeah. I want to know a little bit about Joseph.

Marisa: Okay.

Joe: I'm going to ask the same kind of questions of Joseph as I did of all the authors.

Marisa: Okay. Here's Christ...

(Christ) "Well, first we must, first we must say, first we must say that yes, thank you. Thank you for calling for the personality, the personality of the man, the personality of the man that reared and brought forth what the stories tell as the man that was God, the man that was God, and we say unto you, we say unto you the stories, we say unto you this because they were stories, there were many stories, there were many stories. There are many, many stories.

"What we would like you to do is to put this into perspective. You receive an email. You read the email, and later on in that day, you want to tell what that email was about to someone that you're talking to. You do not remember all the details, so you just kind of tell what it was about. They then – let us just say it was a joke. So you tell the punch line of the joke. You get to that part, but you don't remember if the person in the boat was wearing red or blue or green or if they were with someone or

they weren't with someone, or what they saw or what they felt. You just know the punch line. That person then goes and tells the joke, but they remember more the person was wearing red, this person was wearing green, this person was wearing blue; and because you did not fill in all those details, their mind fills in the details, and then they forget the joke; and then that next person tells it, and on and on and on. And this is all within about 20 minutes of each other. Imagine what happens over 300 years of unintelligent people telling stories to each other about grandiose things that they saw, felt or heard? A simple energy healing that this channel can perform would be considered a miracle in that time. If she was to go into the bible times now, this very moment, she would be considered a high priestess with magical powers. So what one must understand is you must put this into perspective. The consciousness of the planet is going up, and yes, you still get the punch line.

"Someone came down to teach human beings how to live with compassion. That was it. Jesus came to teach people to live from their spirit, not from their mind, and to love themselves and others and to have compassion, and to know and honor the Father or the higher energy within them that is them. This is it, this is all, and this is the basis of many ancient civilization teachings. This is the basis of many teachings. There are many occults, many sects, many religions, quote, unquote, 'religions' that focus primarily on nurturing the spirit, because the spirit is your own individual spirit, rather than 'I have a Holy Spirit' that every single person has, and we all share the same spirit. Yes, we are all One, but we are also individuals. So there are many religions that support this. What the government did not want at that time and what human beings did not have in their consciousness or awareness was that we are God inside. We are clones of God experiencing life in physical bodies that we have created, that we have programmed and lives that we have designed. So in essence, we are God inside. We are God all around us, so just as we have shared (with you) three days ago that the Holy Spirit is a vehicle, we must just have you continue to imagine this within your mind that you are inside the Holy Spirit and you are eternal, whether you want to imagine yourself as Joe or big Joe or whatever you want to see yourself as, see yourself in a bubble that is the Holy Spirit, and inside you have your spirit's personality. That spirit will continue through,

continue through time until you have evolved and ascended. So you must know and you must understand that you are always surrounded by the Holy Spirit, but you are always a Creator God inside.

"Now, we know that you want to ask questions, but we must explain this and reiterate this to you so that you can see and understand how and where all of these quote, 'stories' came from. You must also understand that there are other religions that speak of the virgin birth, the resurrection, the apostles. There are other religions. This is a storyline that has been told throughout all time within the earth plane.

"When entering into the earth plane, it is like entering into a movie that's already been filmed. You look at the movie, you jump into the movie, and you know 'I'm in this movie, so I'm not going to be able to leave Pleasantville,' which is what the movie is. 'I'm not going to leave because it doesn't exist outside of this movie.' There's nothing in this movie that says that there's a Connecticut and there's a Kansas and there's a California and there's a Washington and there's a Tokyo and there's a Japan and there's a Canada (and Peter says, "And New Zealand,") (lol)). There's nothing here that says that there is something that does not say that is here. It is not within the parameters of the movie. If you look back and you look upon the movie not from within it, you can say, 'Oh, that's Pleasantville. There's all these other towns around it.' But when you're in it, when you are in it, you are in it for the rules that were made around the movie.

"So you must understand that the earth plane has rules. The earth plane has programs. The earth plane has information databases within its grid. We have spoken of this grid within (your interview with) John in Revelation about this grid where we play unto the earth music, or we play frequencies, we play sounds within the grid that surrounds the planet and this then affects the rules, affects the people, affects the spirits that are inside the people on all dimensions, on all levels.

"So just as John had said in his Revelations, in your book about Revelation, he had said that if we play rock music in the grid of the planet, no one can hear it, but everyone on the planet will soon begin to

wear rock t-shirts and bash their heads up and down and dance like they are listening to rock music. But then if we turn the classical music on, the classical music will be turned on into the grid of the planet where all the rules and all the stories are placed, and then everyone will begin to get calm, unless they hate being calm and they will get even angrier. So this is what we spoke of about the white horse, about the peace entering into the earth plane. Peace has been programmed into the grid around the planet.

"Now, back to 2,000 years ago. 2,000 years ago peace came at that time and that peace came in the form of our soul family. For our soul family decided to populate a planet that had not been previously populated necessarily by our soul group but very much by beings that were primitive, the beings were primitive. We had only lived on the planet prior (to these primitive beings) to an ancient civilization that were around prior to the earth destroying itself. The Sumerians brought much information into the grid of the planet with many of the rules that were placed. So when one prays and one says, 'Heavenly Father God, please say unto me what I need to hear and tell me what I need to know,' and they see, 'Oh, there's going to be a virgin birth. There's going to be this, there's going to be that, and an angel of God has come to tell me this,' they could either be tuning into the Pleasantville *movie and within the movie that's in the grid, or they could be talking to an angel. So many times when people receive prophecy, many times when people receive information about future events, what they are truly tuning into is a past image, a past story, a past frequency.*

"So we say unto you that many foretold the virgin birth. Many foretold this, and this is what the ascended masters entering into and coming into an earth plane had to play by the rules, so this was something that was needing to be accomplished when entering into the earth. For Mary was trained. Mary was trained her entire life in the works of energy and the works of prayer and the works of rights and rituals and Taoism?

Joe: Taoism?

Marisa: Oh, okay.

Marisa P. Moris and Joseph P. Moris

(Christ continues) "*And understood, understood that from where we all come from, we all return. And this was a one-god concept, whereas there were many Jewish people who still secretly believed in the multi-gods of the Greek era, and many that believed in other more esoteric beliefs such as wickenism – paganism. So you must also understand that when you look upon a movie that you need to go into, let us just say that you, Joe, and this channel (Marisa) are going to go live in a movie so you decide, 'I am going to go live in* Back to the Future*. I'm going to go live in that movie, so I know that I can either be – I can either be Michael J. Fox, I can be the father, I can be the girlfriend, I can be the teacher. I know all of the characters that I can be. Which one do I want to be and which one will be the best for me to accomplish my goal?'*

"*So I, as Christ, chose seven characters to inhabit at that time as a direct line from here, the eighth dimension. So as I stand here in the eighth dimension as a fully charged, a fully evolved spiritual being I projected my consciousness into seven beings at that time. There have been times where I have been up to 25 beings, so I was not necessarily spreading myself as thin as you thought.*

"*So I say unto you that I project myself unto Joseph (Jesus' dad). Joseph was a good man. Joseph was honest. Joseph was a little rough around the edges, and I appreciated that. That was something that I enjoyed and the energy of him was something that I enjoyed playing. He was teased when he was young. He was bullied when he was young. He was a bit small. He was a bit short so many people made fun of him.*
"*Mary was raised as a – as a prophetess, as someone who would take over the line of work that her mother, Jesus' grandmother, Anna, was procuring on the planet, for she was working with the earth grid, for she was working with nature, she was working with divine beings, she was working with the elemental kingdom to nurture the earth with energies to heal people for she made tinctures made of roots. She made many medicines that people would use instead of going to a physician.*"

Joe: That was Anna or Mary?

(Christ)   Anna. Anna taught Mary everything that she knew. Mary knew from a very young age that she was special, and this is not to say that she was special because no one else could do what she did, but this was her mission. This was her plan. She was to bring about the Divine Feminine energy, the Holy Spirit incarnate into the earth plane, and she was to give birth to a being that she would train in all of the same rituals, all of the same energy healing, for lack of a better word, all of the same techniques that she learned from her mother. So this was the plan. When you look at someone and you say, 'Oh, wow, they are a professional baseball player. They have such natural abilities.' Yes, but if the parents were not interested in sticking the child in baseball or they did not nurture or take them to practice or say, 'Go out there and practice even though you don't want to,' then the person would not become a professional baseball player because they would not be in an environment that is conducive to them being a success. So in order for Jesus to be the success in which he was he had to be born to a household that held in higher regards the connection between spirit and God through our own means, not having to go through a Rabbi or somebody that can talk to God but other people cannot.

"So Mary was trained. Mary was trained, and she was not married off. Mary was trained and she was kept in the highest of regard knowing and seeing and understanding that she would be the one that quote, 'played the part' to birth the quote, 'next messiah.' Mary's cousins, aunts, uncles, grandparents, even those from the court wanted to marry her off when she was twelve. She was not married off for many different reasons, but Anna made sure to keep her in virginity. For understand that when children became women, when they began to menstruate, this is when they became women, and this is when they would be married off. This is when they would be given to another man to take off the father's hands, 'Now you have her. She is yours. You take care of her. She will give you babies.' This is the way that women were looked at, and this was the role that they were okay with.

"So she was kept from this for two years until Joseph came along, which was my spirit, my spirit, for understand and know that in order for there to be quote, 'a virgin birth,' in order for there to be something that is procured from nothingness, one must fully understand the spiritual *makeup of spiritual DNA, and we will not go into that, but by combining an angelic force and that which is Mary's higher self in spirit with that which is the T body? The T body of Christ, himself –"* (Marisa: he's talking about himself) *"– within a physical body, much can be accomplished between two spiritual beings without ever having physical contact.*

"So you must understand that everything in the physical becomes physical because it happens in the energy plane first. Your physical body did not exist, but your etheric body did. How did this channel (Marisa) know what her daughter would look like (before and after her pregnancy)? How is that possible? She was not made yet. Is it because she is psychic? No. It is because the etheric body is already created; the life path is already created, the way that she will look is already created, and now that creation, that way that she looks is now in her human field, and due to that, the human field will grow into that. So the human body grows into what the spiritual body is.

"So when one says, 'is that Joseph's child? Is it Mary's?' it is Joseph's and Mary's, and we say this unto you and this is hard to explain, but yes, it is their child, but no, there was no physical interaction to bring the child into the womb. So you must understand this, though. It was still their etheric bodies, it was still their energy bodies, and when trained in the magical rites of that which is the gnostic and the Isis teachings of that day that came together to bring about these magical rites that many would do that were part of these cults, so to speak, were able to bring their vibration and their energy up so high that they were able to either disappear, walk through walls, walk on water. They were able to leave their body, hang out with other people that had left their body, and this is what they did. They had intercourse in the etheric plane, brought their bodies back into their human fields, and then their human was pregnant.

"So understand this and understand this well, there was a child prior to Jesus. This child died. This child was to be a woman, was to be a girl. This child was to bring the information that needed to be brought in order for them to understand and see and know that Jesus was coming. Yes, they were always foretold of Jesus. They were foretold of Jesus

their entire lives, but you must understand that many times because we are blind by the physicality, many times messengers in the form of children that do not survive, messengers in the form of dreams, messengers in the form of angels or deceased loved ones will be sent to the earth plane. If the human beings are not giving the message, many times energies from the other side will get sent down into their field for – to attune the person so that things can take place that need to take place. Does any of this make sense?

Joe: *It makes sense. The only question I've got is, did the child that died, was that from the human interaction or was it the etheric realm interaction that created the child that died? And you said it was a girl, and I'm still confused, because we're under the understanding that it was James, and he died or – yes, that it was a boy. So anyway, that's – I think I understand everything you said, but I still have that little question mark.*

And then also Poochie was growling a little bit. I was thinking a little bit of trying to make sure we were not intercepted by Lucifer in this whole thing, and I just had a feeling like I got bumped, our snow globe got bumped by Lucifer but couldn't get in.

Marisa: *There are some dark angels over there.*

Joe: *I feel like we got a bunch of them all outside.*

Marisa: *Yeah, they are. Can you see them?*

Joe: *I can see them all outside of my Snow Globe.*

Marisa: *They're all like looking in with red eyes.*

Joe: *They're all looking in. They're all looking into our snow globe right now, so keep them out. Christ, keep them out. No holes in our Snow Globes, please.*

Marisa: *Yeah. Christ, he just sent over – it's like a golden pillow deflection. It's like a golden whooshy pillow of energy, and when the angels tune into it, they think they're tuning into us, but it's not us. That's cool.*

Joe: So anyway, that's my question. You mentioned they had a child. Was it Joseph and Mary in the human physical plane that had intercourse and then they had a child that died, or was it like in the case of Jesus who was conceived in the etheric –

Marisa: *"No. That child was in the etheric, in the etheric realm."*

Joe: She was too? Was it a girl?

(Christ) *"She was as well, but she was not born. She was not born, for she brought the information that she needed to bring. What you must understand, let's look at it like this, let us look at it like this: Let's say that you have a computer, and you want to play a song on it. You want to play the Beach Boys. You want to play* Surfin' USA *on your computer. You've heard of it, you know of it, but the computer doesn't know of it. It doesn't understand it. It can't play it. It can't fathom it, because it does not even know what it is. So you cannot just tell the computer, 'Oh, play this song.' It must be programmed into the computer, so you may either find the song on a CD and insert it into the computer and download it onto the computer and then take the CD away and then now it is in the computer even though there is no CD in there, or an SD card or a USB wire to another computer.*

"So what is happening when a child is entering into the womb of a mother is, in essence, information from the upper-dimensional realms is being downloaded into the circuitry or into the energy field of that which is the computer or the person, or the person's spirit. So this girl, Sarah, who then later became the child of Jesus who then also –"

Joe: Wait, wait, wait. Sarah became the child of Jesus?

Marisa: Uh-huh. This is the spirit – oh, it's my guide right here. Hey, Sarah, what's up? Okay. So she's right here.

Joe: *We've made a huge leap here. You're saying that Mary and Joseph conceived a child –*

Marisa: *And it died.*

Joe: *– in the etheric realm, but it never was born??*

Marisa: *"It was never born, for she was pregnant for – she was pregnant for 32 days." Thirty-two days?*

Joe: *So she had a miscarriage.*

Marisa: *Yeah – no, 3.2 months, sorry, not 32 days.*

(Christ) *"Three point two months, for she was not showing, she was not married at this point, at this point, because of this: She was betrothed to Joseph. She was betrothed to Joseph, and they were married, for many people, many people never knew of this pregnancy that she had, because she never showed at all; but what happened was the angel or the energy that is – we will call Sarah, because this is how this channel knows it, this energy, and this is how we have spoken of this energy in past channelings with the two of you – is understanding that this higher-self being or this energy downloaded information into Mary and Joseph's field while it was on the earth plane, and then it left. So understand this, understand this: They had to be prepared, the circumstances had to be prepared for that which is the coming of the Christ energy, for she never believed that it would happen. She never believed that it was actually true. She did not believe that anything like that could happen, and when it did, her panic, her fear and her unworthiness of being the carrier of a child that was to change the world caused her to miscarry. So in order to fully encompass and embrace the responsibility that she was being given from birth and being told from the time she was three years old, she had to experience it first and then have it happen again."*

Joe: *Are you saying then that her stress and her worry caused a miscarriage of a child that was going to be a girl, but it was going to be*

Marisa P. Moris and Joseph P. Moris

a girl messiah?

(Christ)   *"It was to never be born. The plan was to –* *"It was just a download. It was like putting* Surfin' USA *on the computer."*

Joe: So it was to prepare her – by losing the first one, it prepared her for the actual birth of Jesus.

(Christ)   *"And forced her to get married to me, Joseph, Christ."*

Joe: Oh, okay.

(Christ)   *"Forced her to marry me, because –"*

Joe: And it wasn't the same spirit in the girl – what was her name going to be? Was there a name?

Marisa: It was Sarah, but her name is A-L-V-O-K-O-V.

Joe: Okay. So let's keep it simple and call it (the fetus) Sarah.

Marisa: Yeah.

Joe: So the spirit of Sarah was still Christ, but that was a lesson. And then so Christ remained as a spirit.

Marisa: That was not Christ.   That was a different spirit altogether.

Joe: So it's just a lesson to be learned to prepare her for basically the virgin birth that had been created in the etheric realm.

(Christ)   Yes. So it was virgin, but it wasn't virgin. And according to –

Joe: But by human terms, by human, Joseph and Mary didn't have sex, so they didn't have – they didn't conceive of a child here on the earth.

They had that union in the etheric realm.

(Christ)   In the etheric realm, which is just as real as the physical realm, but yes, we understand. From man's eyes, no physical interaction, but from the etheric eyes, from the spirit's eyes, there was still physical interaction and the two of them remember, they felt it, they know it, and this was something that was planned and brought into union together, but in order to come into union and bring their energies together that the way they were, they had to be married."

Joe: So as an aside, and I don't – I hate to go out on tangents, so this is just a minor tangent, and then we'll jump back again – are etheric unions happening in the world today?

(Christ)   "Absolutely."

Joe: There are people on this earth that are considered born by virgin birth?

Marisa: *"Oh, no, no, no. The last one happened was 1962, and – yes, actually yes, 1962. There were 7 in 1954. There was 14 in 1960? There were –" they're jumping around the earth.*

Joe: Where are all these people who were conceived in the etheric realm? I mean, that's done within my lifetime, it's still within my lifetime. Are some of these people on the earth today?

Marisa: *"Many of them are primitive people that need the story of a virgin birth in order to believe and understand the god, so you may find the Bush People out in the middle of nowhere where there is a virgin birth. So you must understand the way to get to a human mind when a human mind is not so intelligent is to do something that is unfathomable to the human mind; and the human mind and the human beings back in that time, it was all about food, shelter, sex, food, shelter, sex, food, shelter, sex. There is not pleasure that came from food. Food was a necessity. Pleasure came from sex. To women it was a duty. This was to bring a child. So to bring a child into the world without having to* have that duty, without having to be with a man, this was something that was just beyond all reason, and this is something that will prove that a quote, 'god exists.' Remember, just like we said, the story of the virgin birth is in the Pleasantville movie. It is already programmed. It is in here.

"So the best way for soul families, soul groups to bring acknowledgement to a greater being than themselves is to just play off the same roles, the same plays, the same movie that keeps playing over and over again. So there is a type of people, there is a path of people, there is a tribe of people that just do not believe in anything else other than their people are diminishing. The souls that are living in them are not being nurtured by their higher selves and by greater dimensional aspects of themselves. So many times, some of the souls will come in and say, 'Okay, well, let's do this. Let's play off this old story that many people have done before, and let's have a virgin birth. Let's have a resurrection. Let's do it.' They plan it, they go, they do it. So it is really, really something that just keeps being done over and over and over, because it's something that continues to wow human beings. Even though human beings will begin to understand as we become more fifth dimensional that the physical body is actually more pliable than the etheric body, because the etheric body is already built. The etheric body is what needed to be downloaded with the information that she needed, because the etheric body is already built into a solid structure that will exist and live for this amount of time with exit points and it will live, it will be married to this person, it will do that. It is programmed completely with the entire movie in it. And to make changes sometimes if one is disconnected, something must be sent down to live inside of it to download the information into it. But understand that 3.2 months of pregnancy and then a marriage, and then seven months later, this is when, this is when Jesus was born unto the world."

Joe: Conceived?

Marisa: "Born."

Joe: Well, that would make sense, because it takes nine months.

Marisa: "*He was early.*"

Joe: He was premature?

Marisa: "*Yes.*"

Joe: So that's why they went ahead and went to Bethlehem for the census while she was pregnant? Because typically a woman who is pregnant would not travel in those days if she was going to be due. So he was born premature then.

Marisa: He was born at – let's see. He was born at – I keep seeing 54 weeks, but that doesn't make sense. Hold on. Is it 54 – 45 – no, that's too much. Hold on. How many months? "Six months." A full six months? "No. Almost six months."*

Joe: Oh, surely a child would have died at six months in those days.

Marisa: Let me see. He was born at six months?

Joe: Let me ask the question.

Marisa: Okay, you ask.

Joe: How many months pregnant was Mary when she had Jesus?

Marisa: "*Six point four months.*"

Joe: Wow. That baby should have died. There's like no way that child should have – I mean even today at 6.4 months, it would have to go into intensive care and be isolated for months.

(Christ)   "*But again, again, this is a miracle. This is a miracle. Miracles needed to be brought unto the earth so those around that did not believe that this was a virgin birth, that did not believe this would say, 'That child should have been thrown to the wolves. That child was weak. That child was born too soon. That child was not born at the*

right time.' It was also to throw off prophecy, and it was also to throw off those who suspected that Mary would get –"

Marisa: Hold on. There're these things trying to get in. Stop it. Hold on.

Joe: I'm just picturing another layer of the Holy Spirit covering our snow globe right now, another smooth layer, another smooth layer just to thicken that snow globe even thicker and thicker. I can see so much darkness outside of our snow globe right now.

Marisa: I know.

Joe: Trying to get in here. Seriously.

Marisa: Uh-huh.

Joe: I mean they want to get in here and just make a mess. Let me ask you: Christ, is this you, Christ? Is what we're learning right now for our highest and best? Is this something that we are going to be passing on to the world, or is this just for our own edification?

(Christ) "This is for your edification, but it is not to say that it is not true, for what we must explain to you and implement into the minds in which you carry in these bodies is that the more you understand, the better a minister you are, because that is what you are. You are a minister of truth. You always have been, you always will be, for this channel is a minister and a teacher and a healer. You are a minister, a teacher and a healer. So what we must say is you cannot be a minister of truth if you do not know the truth. Do you have to share everything you know? No. Does this channel share everything that she knows? No. You share what applies to the person that you're speaking to at that moment. So we want to bring information unto you so that you can fully understand, and then you can then look back on time on earth and see the synchronicities, see all the other times that us, as the same exact spirits playing over and over, just as you have said the other day, recycled souls, continue to live the same stories over and over and over *and over and over on the earth plane within the movie that we call* Earth. *So the understanding that 6.4 months into pregnancy –"*

Marisa: Holy crap. She was pregnant with twins.

Joe: Really?

Marisa: That's what it was. Jesus, did you have a twin sister? Did Jesus have a twin sister? Just yes? No? Ask of the seventh plane, see if he had a twin sister. I think there was a boy and a girl. I think she lost the girl and I think Jesus stayed.

Joe: You're probably envisioning Sarah who was also immaculately conceived with the conception of Yeshua. Eventually we need to circle on back to James again, but –

Marisa: Yeah. No, I know, but Joseph wants to give the story of him. It's like scream – I mean 6.4 months, you add three months to that, that's 9.4 months. That's a regular pregnancy. I seriously think that she was pregnant with two souls, one of a female, one of a male.

Marla: Maybe the masculine feminine?

Marisa: Yeah. The masculine feminine, and then Jesus came in. He was born, and she basically brought down information, like downloaded information and then she stayed in the field, and then she then stayed around and ended up being his daughter. Oh, my God, this is so crazy. Okay. Hold on.

Joe: Leave it for me to ask questions.

Marisa: Okay.

Joe: That way you won't pick up [untranslatable] and we won't end up going in an area where – to be honest with you, I don't want to go.

Marisa: Okay.

Marisa P. Moris and Joseph P. Moris

Joe: It might be true, but I don't want to go there.

Marisa: Where?

Joe: With the twins.

Marisa: Oh. It could be. I mean she could have been pregnant with two.

Joe: It's possible. Yeah, it's possible.

Marisa: I mean, why not?

Joe: Yeah, it's possible, it's true. Okay, I'm trying to decide whether we want to – I mean, at this point I understand how Jesus was born and how he came to be, and that was part of the thing, and we have a little bit that Joseph was a smaller-type person, kind of rough around the edges. It really doesn't matter how he ended up meeting Mary, but they did meet, but it wasn't arranged like normal marriages back then were, so that's a little bit different from custom.

Marisa: Uh-huh.

Joe: Okay ... One child is lost at miscarriage. That was a lesson there. Then Jesus came along, and they now have a young child. At the age of two – before Jesus was the age of two, Herod was trying to kill all the children that were two and under, because the word was out that a messiah had been born, so Herod wanted all the two-year-old's and under to be killed. Mary and Joseph fled and went to Alexandria, Egypt, and they lived there for a while. Is that where they had their next child, which would have been James? I need to get back to the story of James, because we're under the impression that there were two boys born to Mary that were by the name of James and one of them passed away. That's what we understood from yesterday's sessions. So that's where I'm trying to get down to now. Okay. So, Jesus, Mary, Joseph, they've run off. They've gone to Alexandria. Are they now having more children in Alexandria, Egypt?

Marisa: Actually they weren't in Alexandria when they had James.

Joe: Had they returned already to...

Marisa: Bethlehem?

Joe: No, it's not Bethlehem. They lived in – gosh, I'm going blank.

Marisa: Where's Cairo?

Joe: Nazareth. They lived in Nazareth.

Marisa: But where is Cairo? I keep hearing –

Joe: Well, Cairo is in Egypt also, but in those days Alexandria was kind of like the capitol of the world. I mean it's where all the smart people went to and it was Alexandria. They had a great library then, which about three or four hundred years later was burned down during another war and we lost all of earth's history. But anyway, no, Alexandria was a place where Joseph and Mary knew they could go and get lost in the crowd, so to speak plus they had to hide from Herod. So then they came back, I guess, to Nazareth and started the rest of their family, and I'm just trying to focus again back in on James. When was James born in relation to the age of Joseph? We know that Jude was born seven years after Jesus. Where was James born, and was there another James? Was there a James that came first and died? Was there a James that belonged to Joseph before he met Mary? That's where I'm confused. I'm trying to find out the story of James, so I need to be talking to either to Jesus' higher self or I need to be talking to –

Marisa: You're talking to Joseph's higher self –

Joe: Okay, Joseph.

Marisa: – this whole time.

Joe: All of that was Joseph's higher self?

Marisa P. Moris and Joseph P. Moris

Marisa: Uh-huh.

Joe: The whole lesson we've had so far –

Marisa: Uh-huh.

Joe: – has been Joseph's higher self.

Marisa: Yeah.

Joe: Okay but Christ said he was Joseph's higher self. Then Joseph, either way, I'll call him Joseph... Joseph, when did you have your son James, and did you have two boys that were named James?

(Joseph) "Yes."

Joe: What happened?

(Joseph) "Sixteen months after the birth of –"

Marisa: His name wasn't even Yeshua, but we'll call him Yeshua. He's calling himself different, but maybe it's just the different language.

(Joseph) "Sixteen months after the birth of who you call Yeshua...

Joe: Yes, we call him Yeshua.

Marisa: Hold on. Yeah. Hold on. Let me just make sure that I'm in line with this guy over here. There's a dark thing trying to come in over there.

Joe: Maybe we can clear out the snow globe again.

Marisa: Geez, they're like constant.

Joe: I mean I can't even tell you how dark it is outside our snow globe right now. I mean, the glass was perfectly clear. We're sitting inside this beautiful crystal clear snow globe right now, all of us right here in this room, and everything on the outside is just black clouds, just black, black, black, black. They're trying to get in here and corrupt what we're doing.

Marisa: Uh-huh.

Joe: So right now I don't see any darkness in our snow globe –

Marisa: *Yeah, somebody was just coming up behind him, but now he's gone. Okay.*

(Joseph) "Sixteen months, eight days after the birth of our son, Jesus, it was not that much of a shock when –"

Marisa: Hold on a second. I just lost the connection, because that thing kind of went, "snip" and cut my cord with him. Okay. Go back. Okay, so no, Christ says, "No. You need to channel me." So okay, instead of Joseph's higher self. Oh, I thought I was channeling Joseph's higher self. Christ says, "No, you were channeling me."

Joe: Oh, everything we've learned is –

Marisa: *Christ, yeah.*

Joe: Oh, it's got to be, because Christ is the higher self of Joseph as well.

Marisa: *Yeah. Okay.*

(Christ) "Sixteen months, eight days after the birth of what you call Yeshua, there came about another child, another child was born, and that was, that was a girl."

Joe: A girl? How is James older than Jesus?

Marisa: Did Mary have a child prior to Jesus? "No." Did she give birth to a child James? "Yes." So James had a child prior to meeting Mary?

"No." While he was with Mary, he had another child? *"Yes."* What?

Joe: So Joseph had a child with somebody else?

Marisa: While he was with Mary, because she couldn't have – she had to be a virgin. What?

Joe: Oh, so he – well, don't forget. In the olden days, Abraham was with Sarah and Sarah couldn't bear children – oh. He was thinking because Mary had lost their first child, that she was barren but he had to produce an heir.

Marisa: No. She had to stay because of the magical cult, or whatever, the grandmother, she needs to remain a virgin so that blah, blah, blah, this is part of the path. She had the pregnancy and she will have the child, like Anna was like a – Anna, where are you? There she is. OMG, I feel how big Anna is.

Joe: Anna is Mary's mother?

Marisa: Yeah. She is very – not heavy-handed, But Anna said, *"We're here for a purpose."* Anna remembered. Anna said...

(Mary's Mom Anna) *"We are coming here. We're from another planet. We've lived on another planet. It's an evolved planet. We're coming down here to evolve this one. These human beings are small-minded and we need to teach them."*

Marisa: Anna remembered and she taught Mary, but she didn't call them small-minded. Instead, she's saying to Mary, *"You have a responsibility."* And the angels would come and see them, Gabriel and Raphael, and then they had an angel named Michael that would come and see them all the time that they could see.

Joe: They could see and they conversed –

Marisa: Anna could. Mary could see in dreams.

Joe: And Joseph?

Marisa: Joseph could sense and feel when something was different, but he was just a guy. He wasn't very tuned in even though he was Christ inside. So he was there for basically grounding, for bringing some solidity. They were a – so they were a young couple. They were a young couple, and when young couples are together, they are expected to have children. They are expected to created heirs. They are expected to procreate and bring about children into their household. And Joseph's parents expected him to have an heir – not error – an heir. It feels like he had a kid with someone else, because Mary couldn't.

Joe: Was Joseph's parents' wealthy enough to have like concubines or something?

Marisa: Uh-huh. They were wealthy.

Joe: So I'm guessing that he was paired with like a concubine much like – much like Abraham was paired with a concubine who then had Ishmael.

Marisa: No concubine. I'm hearing no on concubine. What's a concubine? Someone that you set your –

Joe: A slave girl.

Marisa: Oh. No, no, no. She was a – let's see. Joseph, will you show me who she was? He says, "She was just a girl." He said she was like a third cousin. They were royalty in a sense.

Joe: Joseph's family?

Marisa: Yeah.

Joe: Were they of the Jewish faith?

Marisa: Not Jewish. They were – not pagan. They were – doesn't feel like they were very religious.

Joe: Well, every –

Marisa: Egyptian, Egyptian gods.

Joe: Okay. They were –

Marisa: Horace.

Joe: Oh, they were following the Egyptian gods.

Marisa: Yeah, Egyptian gods.

Joe: Was Joseph Egyptian?

Marisa: Joseph was, yes.

Joe: Okay. How about Mary?

Marisa: Mary was... Israeli?

Joe: Well, there was no – well, there was the tribe of Israel, and so – okay.

Marisa: So, Joseph had –

Joe: So she was a Jew and he was basically a –

Marisa: Well, she wasn't a Jew.

Joe: – a gentile, so to speak.

Marisa: She was – on the surface she was born to a Jewish family, but with what Anna knew and did and worked with, that was not Jewish, but it was one true god, one true spirit inside and carried all the teachings of the Holy Spirit and one true god and all of that. So the *teachings that Anna taught unto her daughter were many of the teachings that Jesus (Yeshua) then learned and then taught unto the world.*

(Christ) "So you must understand that a child was born into a family that was – if you want to put it like this: Let us just say that Madison was Christ. Madison (Marisa's child) may be born into a family that knows nothing about any spiritual endeavors, anything about energetic uses of the chakras and the bodies and how to transmute energies and use snow globes and all of these things. So she is born into a family that doesn't know anything about this. She would end up more like Joseph. If you bring the same spirit, my spirit, into a child, into a family that openly speaks of spirit, openly speaks of God and having God within and being able to use this piece of God inside, that is when the full acknowledgement of the abilities inside will be shown to the world. So Jesus was taught many things in mystery schools, but much of what he learned was right at home in his early years. So when he was 16 months, 8 days another child was born, and that was a girl. Prior to Jesus being born, two months before, James was born."

Joe: What happened to James?

Marisa: James grew up with him.

Joe: Oh, he did grow up with him.

Marisa: Uh-huh.

Joe: So he was really –

Marisa: Oh wait, hold on. Nope.

(Christ) "The first six years, James was taken care of by handmaidens, handmaidens within the home or the –" they're like showing like a castle "– for Joseph's family, because an heir needed to be procured. His father was sick. He had no brothers. The pressure to have a child to be reared and brought up to take on the family's wealth was something that needed to be established and done. He loved Mary, Mary loved him. They knew they were to be together, but they knew that they had to play the story out. After having had the first child lost knowing that they were pregnant without having been married, without having had relations, they knew that this was real. So he had a child with a third cousin."

Marisa: It's a third cousin. They're like related.

Joe: So did that James end up knowing that Joseph was his father and then –

Marisa: "Ahem, ahem, ahem, ahem (clearing of throat sound)." Here he is. "Er, er, er, erm (clearing of throat sound)."

Joe: Really. The guy with the er, er, er, erm (clearing of the throat sound), is the older James?

Marisa: Uh-huh.

Joe: I thought he was the one that was in the Constantine days that got thrown all the – all the –

Marisa: Let me see. Are you James, older brother? He says, "No. That's him." There's a guy standing right next to him, and he's like –

Joe: So there are two – oh, wait a minute.

Marisa: There's three. There's three James.

Joe: There's three James. Okay. So Joseph had a James with a third cousin who became the heir of Joseph's father's estate.

Marisa: Yeah.

Joe: And he continued to live his life in that estate –

Marisa: For six years, and then he came back and he was raised with Jesus and –

Joe: Joseph and Mary.

Marisa: And, Simon and someone named David.

Joe: So Mary had children by the name of Simon and David.

Marisa: Simon, David, Jude. I think there's a Michael, a Sarah –

Joe: I think there's a Miriam –

Marisa: and Ruth....

Marisa: There's another Mary. She had like nine kids.

Joe: Yeah. Ruth was the last child – according to the Bible, Ruth was the last child of Mary. Okay. So then, there's the older James. He came back at six years, became a part of the family. Something must have happened to the estate.

Marisa: It got taken over by the government. There was war in the land.

Joe: So she ended up having another child somewhere down the line which was another boy, and that one became James the Just? Who was James the Just according to the Bible? According to the Bible, Paul talks about telling some of his followers that they should go talk to James the Just, the brother of Christ.

Marisa: That's his brother that was rich.

Joe: Really? It was the older brother.

Marisa: Uh-huh. Yeah.

Marisa P. Moris and Joseph P. Moris

Joe: So the older brother, James, came into the family –

Marisa: He had a ton of money.

Joe: – and he must have truly believed and followed Jesus then.

Marisa: Yeah. Uh-huh. And he was the one that hired these scribe guys to – hold on. Let me just...

(Elder James) "So I, I believed in the words, I believed in the words of my brother. I believed in the words of my grandmother. I believed in the words of my mother and I believed in the words of my father, for I truly felt and knew inside that my mission was to bring, was to bring the words of Christ –"

Marisa: .... remember, his dad was Christ too.

Joe: That's true.

(Elder James)   "– bring the words of Christ to the world, to the intellectuals, to those who – (urr, urr, urr, clearing of throat sound) – were attracted to the governing forces that were attracted to the high lords, for the pharaohs, the pharaohs that had much money, that had much gold, gold that would drip from their fingers did not want to hear of a love that we have inside of ourselves that will bring you all the riches of the world, for they wanted to impose fear, they wanted to impose their gods, their thinking, their ways. So by bringing what my brother and father and mother shared with us growing up into a world of establishment, this was my part in the role. This was my part in the play."

Joe: This is James?

Marisa: Yeah.

Joe: The older brother that –

Marisa: The quote, unquote, *"Just."*

Joe: James the Just, the older brother.

Marisa: Yeah.

Joe: All right.

Marisa: He – let me see James the Just.

Joe: Just as an aside, I'm not going to put this in the book at all. I'm still going to decide what's going to go in there, but the one thing that was very confusing in The Urantia Book was how Jesus kept referring to James as his eldest brother, and they kept thinking in a way that he was the eldest of all the other children, which meant he was second, but to me the eldest means the oldest.

Marisa: Uh-huh.

Joe: So now it seems to make sense that he would have had an older brother named James.

Marisa: Uh-huh.

Joe: And now I'm getting the idea that the child, James, that saw Jesus healing –

Marisa: That's the younger brother.

Joe: – was the younger James –

Marisa: Yeah.

Joe: – and he was the slow one –

Marisa: Yeah.

Marisa P. Moris and Joseph P. Moris

Joe: – let's not say mentally challenged, but –

Marisa: He was emotionally cute.

Joe: Okay, emotionally cute and probably mentally a little challenged.

Marisa: He wasn't the sharpest tool in the shed, is what Peter just said.

Joe: Okay. All right. Finally. I think it's finally come together. I think we finally got it. Okay. Let's see.

Marisa: Because when Jesus was 16, this James was like 8.

Joe: The younger James.

Marisa: Yeah. But Jesus and James are practically the same age.

Joe: Oh, okay.

Marisa: They're like James is his brother –

Joe: So the older James –

Marisa: – by a few months.

Joe: So the older James became sort of like the father of the family after Jesus left.

Marisa: And he had all the money too.

Joe: Oh, he had the money too.

Marisa: Yeah. He had all the money, because he was –

Joe: What happened to his mother?

Marisa: She was part of the establishment over there.

Joe: So he just – at six years old, he just went to stay –

Marisa: Hold on. Oh, oh, let me see, hold on. Where is your mom? "She died."

Joe: Oh, that's why –

Marisa: Polio or – her skin's coming off. There was a famine – huh?

Marla: Leprosy? Yes. Leprosy? No, no, no, no. Her skin was coming off, and they show all these people all over the city, and a lot of the rich people, because they were eating meat that other people couldn't afford, and there was some sort of like swine illness.

Joe: Oh, okay.

Marisa: – and a lot of the royal people died. So the poor people in town would say, "Thank God that we don't have all that money, because money kills."

Joe: Oh, okay.

Marisa: It was something that went around, looks like for like 10 or 11 months. Looks like it either came from pigs – yeah, from pigs.

Joe: Wasn't cooked thoroughly.

Marisa: It was – the pigs just had a disease or something like that. A lot of them thought that it was a famine from God. Many said, "Oh, God is killing off the rich people because they don't deserve to be alive, but really it was just a common like virus – and yeah, feels like they didn't cook it right.

Joe: Now where was the older James born again? Was it in Egypt or –

Marisa P. Moris and Joseph P. Moris

Marisa: *I keep hearing Cairo.*

Joe: Okay. So they were in Cairo. And this was before Joseph was together with Mary?

Marisa: *No, they were together.*

Joe: They were already together?

Marisa: *They were together, they miscarried –*

Joe: But – so Joseph –

Marisa: *His family said, "You're not going to have an heir for us." The dad was sick. He went and he got with his third cousin from some place. She looks like she should be in* Aladdin, *you know, like she looks very like, you know, like flying-carpet-like, so genie-like, so that would be Egypt, right? So third cousin had a child with him. She gave birth to her child – looks like three months prior to Jesus being born, and it was a boy.*

Joe: Okay.

Marisa: *But then Joseph and Mary had a boy.*

Joe: So Jesus and James were basically almost twins.

Marisa: *Exactly the same age, yeah.*

Joe: They must have been really good friends.

Marisa: *They were really close it shows. But James was not like being a sheepherder and stuff, he was learning how to count money and how to be a diplomat and how to – like it shows him making these little like wooden like cars, like he had toys. Jesus was like playing with a stick when he was little. They didn't have a lot of money, I guess.*

Joe: But James brought some of his wealth even at six years old with him?

Marisa: It looks like the mom died and then Joseph sent – looks like he sent a camel for his son, and the son came to live with them, and the estate was taken care of by someone, but it feels like Joseph had to go there a lot.

Joe: Oh, he was probably negotiating for some kind of a settlement or something.

Marisa: Yeah, he had to go – he had to go back home a lot, so a lot of the times he was away.

Joe: So Joseph was originally from there, Cairo or whatever.

Marisa: Yeah.

Joe: Well, we won't get into the details of how he ended up meeting Mary. We'll just assume it was all meant to be and somehow he –

Marisa: They met at a well, he says.

Joe: What's that?

Marisa: They met at a well.

Joe: Oh, he met her at a well?

Marisa: They were literally – they were traveling. He had this big royalty like, you know, like the coaches and everything, and he was –

Joe: That's how Jesus met Mary Magdalene too....at a well.

Marisa: Really?

Joe: At the well.

Marisa P. Moris and Joseph P. Moris

Marisa: Wow. Instead of bars, they met at wells?

Joe: I guess.

Marisa: Hahaha. Like instead of a pub, they're like, "Hey, let's go to the well."

Joe: You know what? Right now I don't mean to break this off, but it's after noon, and –

Marisa: Do you need to go?

Joe: No not yet but I just want to wrap up. I want to get to Rosemary's take on all of this.

Marisa: Oh, okay.

Joe: And I think that's pretty much going to be it. Rosemary – has she been in here? I don't even need a wrap up. I don't even – well, let's ask Christ again: Is it necessary for us to talk to the older James? Is there any need for us to talk to the older James, because we already know that the James who is the author –

Marisa: He was making fun of you right now. He's making fun of us.

Joe: Who is?

Marisa: Peter.

Joe: Peter, knock it off. Come on. Come on.

Marisa: He says, "We finally get into the truth. We finally get all the juicy stuff. We finally get a connection to someone who's telling us how it is, and you guys – and you guys want to talk to her?"

Joe: Okay. All right.

Marisa: It's Rosemary, and she was like, "Neh."

Joe: All right. Okay, Peter.

Marisa: Peter, be nice.

Joe: Let's get – come on. Peter was not there. Rosemary was not there. Neither one of them were there....

Marisa: ...when they were young.

Joe: ...when they were young, when this was happening. And James, the older James did not go out on the ministry with Jesus.

Marisa: But he recorded all of the beliefs and all of – this is what the older – "Ahem, ahem, ahem (clearing of throat sound)"

Joe: The ahem, ahem, ahem (clearing of throat sound) is the older James, right?

Marisa: Yeah.

Joe: Okay. Does Rosemary know the older James who was considered James the Just?

(Rosemary) "He lived in a different town. We always heard of him. We knew that he had a lot of money. We knew that he was, you know James –"

(Elder James) "Ahem, ahem, ahem (clearing of throat sound)."

Joe: I'm going to ask you the same question, so he can give us his statement as well.

Marisa: Okay. He was like, "Thank God." Peter – he doesn't like Rosemary. Rosemary, why doesn't Peter –

Marisa P. Moris and Joseph P. Moris

Joe: I don't think Peter's ever been fond of –

Marisa: Oh, and Rosemary's like, "I don't like him either."

Marisa: She says, "He's pompous." She's the one with the dress, the poor girl.

Joe: She's our valley girl.

Marisa: She's like a valley girl, and she comes in, she followed Jesus and –

Joe: She's like a Jesus groupie.

Marisa: She's one of my past lives. She's like a fragment of me or something.

Joe: She's really funny most of the time. Was she ever a prostitute?

Marisa: No. She's not really a prostitute – oh, no, no. But she was a prostitute because she got sold into prostitution when she was like 10, and then Jesus saved her or something.

Joe: Well, she found peace through Jesus.

Marisa: So okay, Rosemary says,

(Rosemary)   "Oh, he was just – everyone knew that he had a lot of money, and everybody knew that he was like the brother that could help people out if they were in trouble, because Jesus was like the kind and just one and you could tell him all your problems and he would give you advice; and his brother was more of the one that could give you money if you needed help, but he also knew a lot of lawmen, so when Jesus would help the beggars in the town in which they were from, and many were jailed, he was able to get them out."

Joe: James or –

Marisa: Jesus was able to go to James and say, "Hey, could you talk to your friends over there at the government and let these guys out?"

Joe: Oh, okay.

Marisa: So it was kind of like his government connection or something.

Joe: Oh, okay.

Marisa: Is this true? Jesus, is this true? Yeah? He says,

(Jesus) "No not a government connection. It was more along the lines of people were being thrown in jail for stealing bread, and part of my ministry was that no one should get thrown in jail for having to eat."

Joe: So Jesus would go pay off the bill – so to speak...

Marisa: Yeah.

Joe: ...for the money lost, for the bread stolen.

Marisa: Yeah. And Rosemary says,

(Rosemary) "The coolest thing was that James really did work with scribes and diplomats, and you were mistaken when you thought that he was writing the books with Constantine. The reason why you are seeing him the way that you're seeing him is because when you think of Just, you think of a judge. The reason why you're seeing him that he looks, you're seeing him as a judge. We are trying to bring into you the differentiation between little James and James the Just, duh."

Joe: So are there two James or three James?

Marisa: "There's two James."

Joe: There's two James. So there was not one in the time of Constantine *that became the author –*

Marisa: "There was a James in Constantine."

Joe: Wait a minute. We were told yesterday that he was not named James.

Marisa: "There's a scribe."

Joe: But the scribe wrote the book –

Marisa: Yeah.

Joe: – and put it in the name of James.

Marisa: Yeah.

Joe: Okay. So there are two James and not three James.

Marisa: Yeah, and then there's the scribe that wrote James.

Joe: Okay. And then there's the scribe that wrote the book of James.

Marisa: There's three scribes that wrote James.

Joe: Okay.

Marisa: So the three scribes that were given a bunch of papers, and they said, "Here, put a bunch of rules together and call it 'James.'" Those are the three guys that we talked to the very first time we channeled the author of James, we ended up with those three guys?

Joe: Oh, they were the three authors.

Marisa: Yeah, they were the three authors of James.

Joe: Oh — finally it's all come clear. Thank you, thank you, thank you, thank you, thank you. Does Rosemary want to finish up?

Marisa: *Rosemary says, "Yes, yes, yes, yes, yes, yes, yes, yes."*

Joe: *Let her finish up, and then I want to get Peter's, because Peter and James probably were good friends.*

Marisa: *She says ...*

(Rosemary) *"Okay. So he was the rich one. Jesus was the one that was given the abilities that his mom had and all the knowledge and the – what you would call energy, or the battery, as you call it"*

Marisa: *She's trying to come up with the words that I use.*

(Rosemary) *"He was the battery for Mary. So Mary was a healer. Mary lived forever practically, and Joseph was the one that brought stability to the household. He had to go and live in Egypt a lot of the time, like he would live there for like two years and come back."*

Marisa: *I don't think he died when Jesus was 14. Let me see. Did he die when Jesus was – oh, he did die when Jesus was 14.*

Joe: *Joseph did?*

Marisa: *He got drafted into some sort of military or something.*

Joe: *Joseph did?*

Marisa: *Let me see. Did Joseph get drafted – no. No, no, no, no. Never mind. Why am I seeing him in the military? It's like he was going to do negotiations somewhere, and they got attacked and killed. It feels like he was going to negotiations at a big palace and it feels like their coach and all their horses, or whatever they were traveling on was attacked by like rebel forces or something is what I'm hearing. Rebels.*

Joe: *Like pirates.*

Marisa P. Moris and Joseph P. Moris

Marisa: Yeah, pretty much, for their money and whatever. So he was killed, and that was when Jesus was 14, but prior to Jesus being 14 when he was about 12, that's when Joseph had to start going out to wherever it was that he was from. It's almost like he was like – I don't know. It looks like James was with him and everything too.

Joe: So it had something to do with the maintenance of the estate.

Marisa: With the family estate and James and all that. So he would go out there, but it took 18 days of travel time. So if he left just to go for a day or two, he'd have to travel for 18 days and then he would travel back, so it was like he was gone for like a month and a half at a time, two months, three months, sometimes six months. So it was like he would come back, get Mary pregnant, she'd get pregnant, he'd leave, come back. She liked kids. So a lot of the women from their religion or their cult or whatever they were a part of, Anna's thing, helped raise the kids, so they were raised around a lot of women and respected women greatly.

(Rosemary) "And that's what I love about it, because Jesus just respected women and he just thought that they were just the coolest thing, and since I'm a woman, I think that that was really, really awesome that he tried to bring in the matriarch energy into a society that was not respecting and not admiring women, for we had heard of all the stories of women ruling in Egypt and women having power and when the Jewish faith and the Pharaohs and Caesars took over in ruling the lands, this is when only men were respected. So when Jesus brought teachings in that he learned from his grandmother and then he learned when he went to India, he learned that everyone is equal, and this is one of the teachings, and this is one of the teachings that Ruth wrote about in the book that did not get put in the Bible. So anything that was about women being respected was taken out, anything about women healing, it was taken out. And this is not to make everything about men or women or anything like that, but it's really something that needs to be looked at and not because people should say, 'Oh, now I'm so angry. The Bible's not true,' this isn't true. The Bible is true. Just know that it's not completely complete, and it may be shaded a little bit, but you have to

look at the intelligence of people then." She says, "Look at me. I'm really smart."

Marisa: She just put glasses and a business suit on.

(Rosemary) "I'm really smart, but in those days, supposedly we didn't have a lot of intelligence in our human minds. So –" she says, "And that's why he's a prick."

Marisa: She pointed at Peter.

Joe: Oh, great.

(Rosemary) "He didn't like women."

Joe: Great.

Marisa: Peter's like, "I liked women."

Joe: Okay. Let's finish up with Rosemary and let's –

Marisa: Okay, so Peter – Okay, so Rosemary says,

(Rosemary) "All right. Let him talk. He thinks he's so funny. He thinks he's so funny. He's so funny, yeah. 'I'm Peter and I'm just funny.'" She's like –

Joe: Okay. Peter then. Thank you. Thank you, Rosemary.

Marisa: He says, "Thanks Rose Harry –"

Joe: Oh, my god.

Marisa: – instead of Rosemary!! Hahahaha.

Joe: Oh, my god.

Marisa P. Moris and Joseph P. Moris

Marisa: No, he's funny.

Joe: Peter's a good guy.

Marisa: Peter's hilarious. He's like –

Joe: And so is Rosemary. I don't know.

Marisa: Peter doesn't like Mary Magdalene either.

Joe: Well, he's probably a little bit of a misogynist, but that's okay.

Marisa: He says,

(Peter)   "A little bit." He says, "You can define me by that." He's like, "That's the role I play." He's like, "I was the loud belligerent one."

Joe: Oh, god.

Marisa: He's the angry one. He carried on the role –

(Peter)   "For each of the apostles in this story in Pleasantville *–" (Marisa: they're calling it* Pleasantville *now) "– was one of the characters of six of the human ego, and I was anger and belligerence. So I would be perfectly happy, just perfectly okay and then somebody would say one little thing and I would explode. I would just explode, but everybody knew that I would have my outbursts, and then I would let it go, and then everything was fine. But some of the women just didn't – couldn't get over it."*

Marisa: He's like, "I think they like me."

Joe: Okay. So Rosemary's done.

Marisa: She's like,

(Rosemary)   "I'll never be done, but I'll let him talk, because I can go on and on and on and on."

Joe: Well, this is the end. This is the end of our book. I mean this is the full end of our –

Marisa: She says, "But when are we going to do our book?"

Joe: Well, we're going to do Jesus' –

Marisa: She wants a book.

Joe: She wants her own book?

Marisa: Yeah.

Joe: Maybe we will.

Marisa: We could have The Bible by Rosemary.

Joe: I don't know about that but okay let's get to Peter and wrap it up.

Marisa: So Peter says, "I really do not have much to say, for you have gotten–"

Joe: I just want – let me ask the question. Peter, did you travel or consult or become good friends with James.

(Peter)   "No."

Joe: Okay. So there wasn't a real relationship there. It looks like according to the Bible Paul liked James a lot.

Marisa: Paul and James were close. Paul was into mystical magical arts, and James was very fascinated by all that.

(Peter)   "James did not have the abilities that Jesus and young

James had. Young James – I'm sorry – Jude, Jude had all the same abilities as Jesus, and he didn't need to be taught anything. He just was naturally gifted at healing and prophecy and tongues and all these things that they would do in their house but they wouldn't tell people about it because they were just a nice Jewish family. And then when Joseph came into the picture, they had to be like a nice –" they weren't Jewish.

Joe: Who wasn't Jewish?

Marisa: I'm looking at Joseph. They weren't Jewish. They were – they were like, "We respect the gods," but it's – and they're saying, "gods."

Joe: Oh, that's probably why Jesus never respected the Jewish faith. I mean, he never really respected the hierarchy, the Sanhedrin thing –

Marisa: He's not Jewish, I don't think. I don't think he's Jewish.

Joe: Well, everybody supposedly was Jewish back then.

Marisa: Just like everybody's Christian?

Joe: Yeah.

Marisa: Kind of? Or, you know, like the country is mostly Christians.

Joe: Yeah, but Jesus never had a good thing to say about the Pharisees and the Sadducees and the Sanhedrin.

Marisa: Well, the story about the – the story about his dad falling off a ladder or whatever is not true, and he didn't hate Lot, and he didn't hate people with money.

Joe: Jesus?

Marisa: No – because he had money. He could have as much money as he wanted, because his brother had money.

Joe: Oh, okay.

Marisa: And when Joseph died, it's like Jesus and all the kids got like half the money, and then like James got the other half, or something.

Joe: Okay. Just to – I think we're wrapped up.

Marisa: So Peter says, "Okay, okay, okay."

Joe: I do have one question of Peter though –

Marisa: Okay.

Joe: – before he wraps up. Peter, did you attempt to walk on water?

(Peter) "Yeah, I did it a lot of times."

Joe: Really?

(Peter) "Yup, I probably did it – once I learned how to do it I needed somebody there with me. I needed either a woman who had very strong energy or I needed Jesus. I needed somebody there that believed in me and knew that I could do it."

Marisa: He did it 7 or 11 times. Seven times? Eleven attempts, seven he did it, the others he just fell through.

Joe: Wow. Hahaha. That is so cool. That is really, really cool.

Marisa: You really, really walked on water, like for real for real? Your etheric body did? He goes,

(Peter) "Nope. Physical body. You would be surprised what you can do with energy here. You guys are so blind, but that's okay, because that's what we are when we're in physical bodies, but your physical body is not even physical. It's just, it's just an energy body that's a little bit more dense so your eyeballs can see it and you just think it's dense, but

really we can walk right through you, and you can walk right through anything, because you're in a movie. So as people begin to understand their multidimensionality, as this channel would call it, they will begin to realize the abilities and the miracles that can be created. Sickness can be plucked from somebody's energy and removed. They can heal. People can walk on water. People can walk through walls. It is really, really all just mastering the etheric energy body, which is the true body."

Joe: Wow. What a perfect ending to the Bible series books.

Marisa: Cool. Thanks guys!

Joe: That's really good. Thanks Jesus and everyone else!! What about Judas?

Judas

Joe: I'm glad he came in. What time is it? It's only 11:30, so let's ask Jesus, if it's okay--this is kind of spooky. I'm a little nervous about this--ask Jesus if it's okay if we interview Judas to wrap up this book.

Marisa: I don't like this one. I don't like him.

Joe: Judas? Don't do it then. Judas is the one that "backstabbed" Jesus...

Marisa: He just walked in. He's holding a knife in his hand. He's going like this. He's very scary looking. But is he just coming in looking scary? Was he supposed to be scary? Hold on. Let me see.

Joe: Let's just ask Jesus if it's appropriate to talk to him. Jesus, do you want us to interview Judas and add this to this book?

Marisa: No.

Joe: Okay. Then let's stop. Because I don't want negativity in this book.

Marisa P. Moris and Joseph P. Moris

Marisa: He says, Judas will say bad things because he's jealous.

Joe: Okay. Let's not do it.

Marisa: He says that his view of things would be skewed differently. Hold on. Let me just make sure. Jesus, are you sure that you don't --? He says, "I am sure." Who is Judas?

Joe: You're asking me?

Marisa: Yeah. I'm asking you.

Joe: Judas is the one that sold Jesus out. He's the one that took 36 pieces of silver to tell the Romans where to capture Jesus.

Marisa: Oh, no wonder he has a knife in his hand.

Joe: Yeah, to literally stab Jesus in the back.

Marisa: He's got long black hair to right here. He's missing a few teeth right here. And he's got a knife. He looks like a pirate; he looks like a pirate. You know, with like the missing teeth, and he's got the knife, and he's got --. Yeah, he's not a good guy. Isn't Judas his brother?

Joe: No, no. You're thinking of Jude.

Marisa: Oh, I thought you said Judas was his brother.

Joe: No, no. Judas was one of the apostles. And Judas felt – and I'll just tell you what I understand--Judas felt like Jesus should be a king like David and was upset that he wasn't a warrior instead of a pacifist.

Marisa: Right now, he's saying right now, Judas is saying that putting false beliefs in people's heads and making them believe that you're something that you're not is not something *that is godly or just, because it's blasphemy. He's saying that he saw something that --. Everybody said that Jesus was so pure, but he saw him do something, so he's going to start smearing Jesus.*

Joe: I don't want to go there then.

Marisa: He's going to start smearing him. And he's lying, too, is what Rosemary says. But what do they say that Judas did?

Joe: The understanding by theologians is that Judas felt that Jesus should have been more like King David, because the Jews were expecting another warrior to sit at the throne of the Jews, and to wipe out all the enemies of the Jews.

Marisa: Oh, but he (Jesus) was all loving and kind.

Joe: But Jesus was of love and he was very sedate, and he was anti-violence. And Judas wanted Jesus to be like a king.

Marisa: Oh, no wonder Judas has the knife and the "Grrrr."

Joe: That's why he turned him in. He was mad at Jesus. He was mad at him because he was --- from my understanding, from my learning throughout Christianity, and this is what I've been taught, so take that with a grain of salt, but what I've learned was that Judas was jealous of Jesus.

Marisa: Yeah, he's very jealous.

Joe: Because he felt that if Jesus gave him the ability, then he would be the king. Judas would be the king. He would get to sit on the throne, and tell everybody what they can do and kill all the enemies of Jesus and the apostles. But he didn't really respect Jesus because Jesus wouldn't take up arms and be a king like what Satan wanted him to be. Satan told Jesus, "All the kingdoms of the world are yours. Just bow down to me." And Jesus said, "No, get behind me." And Jesus was like a lamb. He was not like a lion. Judas wanted Jesus to be like a lion.

Marisa: Judas is coming in. I don't understand. So Jude is Jesus' brother, but Judas, why did you ask about Judas in this book then? Oh, because he's an apostle.

Joe: He was an apostle.

Marisa: Oh, okay.

Joe: And I asked him because this was going to kind of be the last book, and I said, "You know, I wonder if we should ask Jesus if –"

Marisa: Judas says that he saw Jesus in front of a prostitute house.

Joe: Judas saw Jesus in front of –

Marisa: In front of a prostitute house giving someone money, and he was sure that Jesus was, you know, with the prostitutes, and he sees now that he was not now that he's dead, but he was angry about it then. I guess he was giving someone money. I mean, he's really giving a prostitute money or something. He says – he's showing like this house with all these women in it and he has a bag of money and he's giving money to someone, and when he saw that…. He has a knife, huh? Okay, Judas, back off. Anyway yeah, that's what Judas is saying that he saw.

Marisa: Judas says it wasn't even that. He's saying that he was promised something.   He was promised --.   He was promised something but --.

Joe: Who promised him something?

Marisa: The government officials, but they didn't --. It's like they --. He's a bad guy, but I don't think he thought Jesus was going to get killed. I think that he thought, it's like he was jealous of him and he was mad at him because he saw something. It's almost like Jesus was helping a woman that he liked, or something. Judas liked a woman, or something, and Jesus was talking to her, and everybody was like, "Oh, Jesus!" And he keeps saying, "I didn't think they were going to kill him."

Joe: That's why he hung himself. He committed suicide.

Marisa: Yeah, he has a rope around his neck. I didn't want to say that.

Joe: So he was hung.

Marisa: Yeah. He hung himself? Yeah, that's what I saw. I didn't say that.

Joe: On a tree.

Marisa: Remember I said that he had the knife? Right now, that's why I thought I was nuts, but right now, the reason why I say I saw a knife is because he cut himself off the tree. And he has like a rope around his neck and he looks really creepy and he has no teeth. I didn't want to say he's a dead guy. He's an earthbound spirit.

Joe: Did he think that if he turned Jesus into the authorities and was arrested, that Jesus would then rise up like a lion and overtake, rather than --?

Marisa: Yeah, he (Judas) kind of thought that if he (Jesus) was tested, he (Jesus) would show them (the Sanhedrin) what he had. Show them (Sanhedrin) what he got. "I dare you take me."

Joe: So Judas did believe in the power that had been given to Jesus by God.

Marisa: Yeah. He believed in Jesus. He believed his entire life that Jesus was going to come and then he came, and he believed in him, but it's like.....he's not being very clear. He's kind of blubbering. But at the same time he's saying he loved Jesus, he loved him like a brother. It's like he didn't......it's like something took over him and he didn't know it was happening, and then it happened, and then it was done. It's almost like an entity took over him.

Joe: Wow. Okay, well Jesus already said no, we better not add the negativity.

Marisa: Yeah, but it's because he's an earthbound spirit. It's because he hasn't crossed over.

Joe: He still has not crossed over? Jesus has not allowed him into heaven yet?

Marisa: No, Jesus doesn't keep anyone out of heaven. He just....this is the aspect of Judas....

Joe: Oh because he committed suicide, and he still retains all his human emotions.

Marisa: Yeah.

Joe: Okay, which means he can lie readily.

Marisa: He can. It's not even that he's going to lie. He's just going to tell us how he feels and how it is. He is a lot easier, actually, to connect with than....

Joe: Can we tell him to go on? Cross over, Judas. Go. See the light? Go. Quit condemning yourself. God's going to love you.

Marisa: So what he says is – Jesus and him want to clarify

everything, which could probably be put into one paragraph. Judas loved Jesus. Judas was a follower of Jesus. He always looked up to and was waiting for – he was always told the stories – I think he was Jewish – of how somebody would come along and save the people. His mom feels like she was – I don't know, a slave or some sort. Not a slave, but maybe all women seemed like slaves then. His mom was real repressed. His dad was a warrior and he was kind of a scholar like he would read the old religious texts or whatever it was they had at that time and he would pray that someday he would feel or know God. So he's showing Jesus, he's showing himself sitting like at a table eating somewhere and Jesus is kind of across the way. And then I just kind of see Judas walking up to Jesus and then I see him joining the group, or something like that. That's kind of like what I see. But then it shows about two weeks in, anytime Jesus would say anything that didn't seem Godlike, it would like smash all of his dreams, like his image of Jesus was being distorted. He says,

(Judas) "And then there was this woman, Cass –" Casstrinomy? I don't know what her name was, but it starts with a C –

(Judas) "There was this woman, a woman that I loved dearly. She was oppressed too by the government and by the men around her. I loved her. I wanted to betroth her. I wanted to betroth her, but I felt that since I was part of something great that I did not have time for this."

Marisa: So it's like he finally became a part of this God revolution, the Messiah, all of this and was all mixed up in this, but he loved this girl. And he says he was walking by and I see him eating like blueberries or something like that. I see him walking by, and he's got like his knife hanging off the side of him. I don't know if he really has that or not, but it's a big huge hatchet thing and Jesus is handing the woman that he loves money in a bag and he like loses it and he says ...

(Judas) "Twenty-seven days pass – twenty-seven moons and suns pass and the anger grew deeper, for all I could think was that Jesus was not who he said he was and was oppressing the one that I loved."

Marisa: And then it just shows him going to the government and saying something and then the next thing I know Jesus is getting killed and Judas is killing himself or something. So it's over a woman.

Joe: Oh, okay.

Marisa: But Jesus was helping her. Let me see. Who here can tell me – Peter. Peter says – Peter says,

(Peter) "People give us money all the time in the ministry. People donated money and gave money, and many times we would – for lack of a better word – donate money to families or causes, and this is the case with what Judas saw."

Marisa: Interesting. There's so many holes in this story. I can see all the holes in the story. They're not telling me everything, but I think the basic fact of the matter is it was over a woman.

Joe: Oh, a misconception of –

Marisa: Misconception over a woman and Judas felt – feels like a – that he got jealous and he got upset and his image of Jesus was shattered. Yeah. Peter says …

(Peter) "That's pretty much it. Yeah, you got it, you got it. That's pretty much it."

Joe: Oh, okay.

Marisa: Yeah, it's like his eyes --. The reason I thought he looked like a pirate is because he looked like Johnny Depp with all the black eyeliner. His eyes are all black, and he looked sad, and he's crying. I think there's a piece of him that hasn't crossed over, but I think that his higher self is --- hold on ... Jesus says that there're pieces of him that have been left behind in that time and because we're tuning into those pieces of him, that's what we're talking to but that the greater totality of who he is, has crossed over and he's fine.

Joe: Okay. Let me ask Jesus then. Jesus, when you chose Judas to be one of your apostles, did you know then, right then and there, that he was going to be the one that would betray you?

(Jesus)   No.

Joe: Did you know you were going to be betrayed at some point? You had to, because the Old Testament.

(Jesus)   Twenty-three days before.

Joe: Only days before?

(Jesus)   Twenty-three. But I knew that my life would have to come to an end because ... I was told by the greater spirits.

Marisa: Well, isn't that what he just said? Isn't that what Judas just said?

Joe: What?

Marisa: How many moons and suns? Twenty-three moons and suns or did he say 27?

Marisa P. Moris and Joseph P. Moris

Joe: Yeah, yeah, I think he said 27, but –

Marisa: Interesting.

Joe: Wow. Okay. Jesus found out 23 days before he died but maybe Judas started planning it 27 days before.

Marisa: Judas saw him with the money. Judas saw him do the money thing 27 days before.

Joe: Oh, okay.

Marisa: And then Jesus probably heard about it and probably started to suspect something. Okay. Interesting.

Joe: Yeah it was kind of foretold in the Old Testament anyway. And when we get into the Old Testament, if we do a book on the Old Testament, we'll talk to Daniel and Isaiah and some of the other prophets, like Jeremiah, who had foretold Jesus' coming, even down to him riding on a colt before he was -- riding a colt into the town-- when he knew he'd eventually get arrested. Okay, let's wrap up this session tonight with Rosemary. Let me just ask Rosemary, what her take of Judas was when she saw him, when she saw him among all the other apostles, before he turned Jesus in. Did she have any inclination that he was kind of like an outcast among the group? What was her take on Judas prior to Jesus' being arrested by the Romans?

Marisa: She says,

(Rosemary) "I didn't really know Judas, I didn't like him, and I didn't want to know him."

Joe: Okay. Good answer.

Marisa: She says that she knew of him. She just pointed to a lady named Sarah. Looks like Sarah was his wife.

Joe: Judas' wife?

Marisa: Yeah, it's another Sarah. It's not --.

Joe: Just a "Sarah"?

Marisa: A Sarah, yeah, and she's crying, and she says that it was like a childhood fantasy like belief that, you know, he would come save the world.

Joe: Judas would save the world?

Marisa: No, that the Messiah --.

Joe: It was a boyhood fantasy that he would be alive at the time of the arrival of the Messiah?

Marisa: Yes.

Joe: And so he obviously must have been thrilled when he had the opportunity to be a part of the inner circle of Jesus.

Marisa: Yeah.

Joe: So that is what pissed him off because he didn't turn out to be the messiah that he anticipated.

Marisa: Yeah, well this lady, she's saying, she says,

(Judas' wife Sarah)   "He's really a good man, a good man. People need to understand he was a good man. But he had to play the part. He had to play the part. Now that we're over here"— (she's talking about spirit) — "We know that everybody played the part that they needed to play.

Marisa: Judas was married to this woman, Sarah, but his first love was a girl who now is like in prostitution. He had a

child with her and Jesus was giving money to her to take care of the child because he loved Judas so much. So Jesus was over at like this place that looks almost like a brothel but all the women had their kids there and he has this big bag of like, you know, silver, or something. He's handing it to the woman. She's like, "Oh, thank you, so much," and she gives him a hug and he walks away; and I can see him, he's just all like clean and white robes, and she's all like dirty and gross, but she's got two kids next to her which is a little girl and a little boy, and they're all dirty with like mud all over their face and you know, look all hungry and stuff. And those were Judas' like bastard children.

Joe: Jesus was giving money to Judas' bastard children?

Marisa: The woman that Judas had children with and he saw him do that, and 27 days later is when Jesus got killed.

Joe: Oh.

Marisa: He saw him giving her money and thought it was because he was like trying to be with her or something so he let human emotions take over.

Joe: So he was married but he was seeing Jesus with someone that he had had –

Marisa: He had had children with or secretively, nobody knew about it.

Joe: Oh, okay.

Marisa: And that's why –Judas, did you think that about Jesus? He says,

(Judas) "Jesus didn't even know about them, or so I thought."

Marisa: So that's why he thought it was so weird that Jesus was over there giving this woman money that supposedly is kind of like a prostitute or something.

Joe: Right.

Marisa: And the kids are standing there maybe it's just a depiction that he had these two kids. Did you have those two kids with her? He says yes. He says eight years prior to this happening he had had a boy and a girl, like twins. He had spent an evening or a day with her when Sarah was sick. So he had been with Sarah for 12 years, and he slept with this woman that he was in love with prior to that before and had bastard children. So he had never – he said – let me see ... Judas, had you ever told Jesus about the bastard children?

(Judas) *"No. And this is why I thought – I don't know...I just got so mad. I don't know if I was ashamed of myself for knowing that somebody knew. Looking back at the way that humans are spirit living in a human at that time, I realize now that most of it was just human guilt and shame for realizing and knowing that somebody knew, because the only people that knew were my sister, and that's it. My sister."*

Marisa: He was afraid that someone was going to find out. So what Jesus is saying is Jesus says,

(Jesus) *"So as we bring truth, as we bring truth to the light, it brings about a better understanding, brings about a better understanding, because what you can see is you'll see many, quote, "characters" in here that you will see as holographic images –"*

Marisa: He's talking to me.

(Jesus) *"But this is because these are characters, like if you were to say, 'Oh, there's Batman,' Batman will come in, because Batman is a created character. So there are created*

characters and then there are actual spirits, and then there are actual consciousness that you speak to whereas you're speaking to my consciousness or the spirit that I was as Jesus right now, but you look upon there –"

Marisa: And he's pointing up and he says,

(Jesus) *" – and then you see the consciousness that I am, which is the Christ consciousness. You look upon Judas and you see the spirit that he was, and this is a fragment that broke off from him, but now when you speak unto him, you are speaking unto the higher self that was Judas."*

Marisa: *Now I'm talking to Judas. He's like on another planet. So he says, Judas says,*

(Judas) *"Metaphorically, if you look at this, you can see that guilt, shame, fear of being transparent is what kills the Christ within. So if you look upon this now and you look upon this metaphorically and you say guilt, shame, fear of being transparent killed the Christ. This was the lesson which we are bringing to the world."*

[NOTE: Small interruption.]

Marisa: *I was just channeling Jesus. Good thing I can channel in the middle of craziness. So he says – we're talking to Judas right now. Yeah, of why he turned Jesus in. So he says – so Jesus says,*

(Jesus) *"If you can look at each one of these stories and you can look at each one of these tales, you can truly see at the emotional level what all of these lessons were for. If you look at Judas, you look that he was discovered, something was discovered that he had hidden deep inside. He was a prideful man in the sense that he always wanted to do God's work. He always wanted to grow up and be a part of something great, and then he succumbed to human instincts. He succumbed to instincts of man, went outside of the home of the one that he was betrothed to and unto that brought about what you would call bastard children. But we must say unto you that each one of the stories that we tell, each one of the stories that we tell within the* Book of Life, *as James called it earlier, the* Book of Life *are stories that can be looked at an emotional level. Everyone looks at this as more of on the physical level where he turned him in, he's a bad person, he got Jesus killed; but what many don't realize and see is that yes, yes, just as we have just mentioned in this transcription that you are reading, Joe, is that there was a plan. There was a plan, and this was to be enacted, just as you have a plan, just as your daughter has a plan, just as – just as –"*

Marisa: (He said Poochie)

(Jesus) *"– just as Poochie has a plan, everyone has a plan. So to feel sorry for me, to feel bad for me, to say, 'Oh, poor Jesus. He died on the cross,' this is something that is unnecessary. It's to look at these lessons and to look at the teachings in which I brought. The teachings that I brought were compassion for Man. There was no compassion at this time when I chose to incarnate. There was no compassion. It was survival of the fittest. It was – it was every man for himself, and truly men, yes, they would take care of the women, because the women were pregnant and they were having children, but many of the women were completely oppressed in the Jewish faith. In the religion in which I was raised in, in the belief system in which I was raised in, women were powerful, women were matriarchs, women deserved respect. So what we brought in was an understanding that women and men alike are just as important in God's eyes and can bring about a change on the planet. When I taught this alongside Mary and my mother –"*

He's calling her Mary, but he calls her Maryam.

(Jesus)   *"Maryam and my mother."*

Joe: Maryam was one of his sisters.

Marisa: No. Maryam – he's calling Mary Magdalene Maryam. Yeah.

(Jesus)   *" – alongside Maryam, we brought about something that scared the Jews, that scared the government, that scared the men, because we said that women are just as powerful, women bring life, bring birth, bring us into existence, but not only that, they have the energy and the love of the Holy Spirit naturally within them. Men have to dig for it. Women can naturally encompass this and pull this from within."*

Marisa: He's saying that's like the intuition or something. He says,

(Jesus)   *"So if you start to look at this, just take yourself outside of these teachings, Joe. Take yourself outside of these teachings and just look at this, look at this not as – not as a Bible, not as a text written by God, not as anything that is sacred, and just look at the stories and how they've been placed in here, and look at them metaphorically and look at the emotions and the feelings that come behind each one of them. You will see that each one of the apostles or the – yeah, the apostles that are mentioned all carry a characteristic of the ego that the human mind is made up of. Each of the stories in the Bible always have something to do with an ego characteristic squashing out – for lack of a better word – the spirit inside or the Christ within. So what we are bringing forward today, what we are bringing forward today is an understanding of, yes, Jude, James, my brother, yes, I had two brothers named James, what you must understand is that even though I died fairly young, my mother lived to 102 years old."*

Joe: Wow. Wow.

Marisa: What?

Joe: Wow.

(Jesus) *"My mother lived to 102 years old. This was unheard of. This was something that no one could ever possibly imagine. In fact, she took on a different name after a while because she wanted her identity hidden."*

Marisa: What? Okay, hold on. Back up. Am I – is this Jesus? He says,

(Jesus) *"It's me. It's me."*

Marisa: Okay. So Mother Mary lived to 102? What about Joseph? "87." That's like an ungodly amount, like back then.

Joe: Uh-huh.

Marisa: Why did they live so long?

(Jesus) *"They knew how to preserve, they knew how to heal the human body, and they knew how to bring etheric matter into form. My mother knew how to make tinctures. She knew how to make medicine. She knew how to heal by touch, and this is where I learned this when I was young. Many of my brothers and sisters carried the natural abilities that my mother carried, and in her divine plan she chose to stay on the earth and have children and pass along the teachings that she so loved and desired and the teachings that I taught. The teachings that I taught are not Christian teachings. They are the teachings that my mother and my grandmother passed down to me and my brothers and sisters. They are the teachings that we learned from our one true God, that we are spirit in human bodies, and we need to appreciate and love our human bodies, and we need to nurture our human bodies and live happy lives and not be afraid of a wrathful, vengeful god. We on a regular basis in our home heard from angels, because*

my mom and my grandmother spoke to them. They spoke tongues and they brought through valid sacred texts and information that we all learned about."

[End of transcription – 6 – Jesus at the Very End – 20 Mins or So]

Marisa: And Jesus is saying ...

(Jesus) *"Just as your father" – [he's talking about Grandpa Joe]— "played the part he needed to play, everybody plays the part they need to play to add to the human consciousness and awareness that God is God. And god is within each of us. So we each had a role, but we did not necessarily know what that role was when we were in human form, because we did not remember what that role was (after birth). But, prior to entering into the matrix of earth we knew what those roles would be. So yes, at a soul level we all knew, we knew the plan, we knew the play, we knew the idea of what would be happening, we all planned it, we all went in knowingly what would happen but once in, just as both of you know ...*

Joe: We don't remember ...

(Jesus) *... we don't remember. But that aspect that does remember, that piece of us that resides within us that remembers all, is the reason why we did what we did, so that each and every human being living at this time could know that you are god, you carry god within you, and you create your life the way that you would want god to create it, the way that you would love it, the way that you would want it to be. So when you ask upon the Father, when you ask upon that god-source within you, you know that you are the one that created this life, you are the one that created all this, and to look onto it and even say 'oh, my angels or my guides will make this happen,' you must say and must know, and you must know at the very deepest, deepest, deepest* *part of your being, that you are the one that instructed these guides to help you to do this. So you must know and understand and see the power that you carry within, the power that you carry within you and around you. So know that each and every day that you breathe a breath, know that each and every day that you breathe life into that beautiful, divine body in which you live in at this time, know that we are all one, yes, and we say this a lot, and nobody truly understands what this means, but if you were to truly, truly embody that which is the one, which is God, we would all be the same, we would all be the same person, we would know all of the same things. And, you do know all these things. So know, each of the two of you, understand that as you continue to have these conversations with us, as you continue to have these conversations, you will see and you will understand that the awareness that is brought about you is growing, the awareness that is brought within you is growing. And your life will change. Your life is changing. And you will see that much more light is brought within you to carry throughout unto others. For others may feel disruptions in their life because of your light. For many of the things that they do not deal with on a day-to-day basis, you come into their life and these will be uplifted in their life, and they will begin to deal with these things, and go through things that they have not gone through at a much faster rate than they have. For, the two of you are healers and you bring this light into each other's and those around your lives. So be patient, be kind and understand and know that you are bringers of light, you are ministers of truth, and we are proud. We are proud of the two of you. We bless you and bid you a good night."*

Joe: Amen. Thank you, Jesus.

Marisa: He just walked away. This time he had a lamb in his hands.

Joe: Thanks Judas, thanks Sarah, thanks Rosemary, thanks to both James.

Marisa P. Moris and Joseph P. Moris

Marisa: *Thank you, council.*

Conclusion to the Bible Speaks books I-IV

I just deleted about three pages of what I thought was the conclusion, my conclusion, after interviewing the authors of these timeless books from the Bible. After three typewritten pages I realized that I cannot possibly summarize best what everyone will learn or glean from the words and lessons we've been taught.

All I can admit to is being a searcher for some kind of truth while I was growing up. Church was the furthest thing from my mind. But I sure was curious about strange things on earth and in our universe. I read a book by a very close friend of Albert Einstein's when I was in college. It was called *Earth in Upheaval by Immanuel Velikovsky.* Velikovsky's book tried, through the examinations of the world's religions and cultures to explain the causes of strange earthly phenomena such as reverse polarized rocks, enormous mountain ranges being geological infants and other phenomena.

One hypothesis which piqued my interest was when Velikovsky discovered ancient Polynesian lore that said at the time of great war in the sky the sun did not rise for three days. Upon his further discovery the time of this occurrence coincided exactly with the sun standing still for three days in the time of Joshua from the Book of Genesis. This, to me was my first curiosity about the Bible in that maybe, just maybe it was an historical text. I ended up reading the Bible from cover to cover but it didn't make me a religious person. I found the Bible to be a good story but that was about it.

It wasn't until I read another strange book entitled *The Urantia Book (no author)* that I became interested in the Bible a second time. That was in 1998. I read it a second time and found myself being baptized in the name of Christ right along with Marisa. I felt the Holy Spirit come upon me but Marisa did not. Marisa talks about her journey as well as I talk about mine in our first book, *Answers Heaven Speaks*. In summary, I embarked upon a journey to find Christ but I just still couldn't figure out just who Jesus was. Marisa still didn't have a clue for she was not religious at all. Her foray into the world of interdimensional contact will be featured in an upcoming book co-authored with noted author and publisher, William Gladstone. I hope you'll watch for the book *I am Marisa*. You'll love it.

I bring that brief bio up because Marisa and I like to reiterate that neither of us are theologians. We're both seekers of the unseen and unheard yet there. Our discovery led to understanding the meaning of our lives. We think that your journey with these authors will bring forth more joy and understanding when you read the Bible. But, even if you aren't a big Bible sort of person, hopefully these conversations with these extraordinary historical figures will give you a better understanding of your relationship with God, the Light, the Source.... whatever you want to call the most Supreme Being that we all know is there.... but we just aren't quite sure. This brings, as they have told us, a sort of quantum physics college course down to a kindergarten level so that we can understand God's complexity yet also his simplicity.

Personally, Marisa and I discovered Jesus, the Christ, the Yeshua, the creator of all souls. We have come to have a very personal relationship with him that is very unique but shouldn't be. Just believe us when we say he's really a nice, down to earth guy when you get to know him. Here's a fitting close to the Bible Speaks series. Only Jesus can conclude these books.

Epilogue
Jesus Speaks

(Recorded 2-13-2015)

Joe: Should we do an interview with you and include it now in this second book (series) of ours? We want to do a book just on you, Jesus. We've already got a ton of him in these authors' books already.

Marisa: He's walking over. He says---

(Jesus) "You may do unto this (next) book what you would like to do, but I place before you my words, I place before you my honor and I place before you my knowledge in that which I can bring to you. For I can bring it to you as Yeshua the man; I can bring it to you as Christ, that which is the Holy Christed being of God; I can bring it unto you as the spirit of man, and I can bring it to you as God. So you must first understand what you would like to be telling the world in this next book. For you may interview me, you may ask me questions about who I am, and what my life was about, but there are many speculations about my life already and who I was, and what I did. But bringing about the examples, bringing about, as they say, parables to explain to people who they are, why they are here,

where they are going, where their loved ones are, where they are going in their life, are different ways they can learn to live a life in an honest fashion, but also live with the love of God within their heart, understanding and knowing that love is unconditional, love is light, light is ever withstanding to that which is darkness.

So know and understand that this will be a ministerial book indeed in that people will read it to feel good. People will read it to understand. People will read it to say, 'Oh, that's what they mean. Oh, Jesus was the man, His higher self was Christ. I understand this now. Oh, this is understandable for I understand, and I understand as a man.

I, Jesus, lived this life not knowing who I was or where I was going, or where I had come from. And, I was told exactly, told exactly where I came from and where I was going, but I still did not believe, for I was a man. And just as each person is told on this planet: 'You are here for great things. You are here. You are god. You are a creator. You're a co-creator of God and you can create whatever you would like.' But does anybody know what they want to create? Gosh, no. They do not know because they do not know why they are here. So if they were to understand the inner workings of the way that things are structured, if they were to understand the inner workings of their soul, of their soul body inside, and know how they can create a life of their dreams, this is something we would like to bring through.

Yes, we can interview me about my life. We can interview those who surrounded me. But know and understand that I brought ministry to a world of darkness. The two of you bring ministry to a world of darkness. And I would love to be a part of bringing this ministry, of bringing this happiness, of bringing this joy, of bringing this faith, and bringing laughter to the world; the world that does not know much laughter. We will bring the joy and the peace and the reverence to a world that feels as if it has no hope. For, we can bring examples, we can bring these parables into people's lives so that they may truly understand why they do the things they do, why they feel the things they feel; why does a wife get angry at her husband? Why does she get angry? Why does a man get angry? Why do they think that the world is coming to an end, when their emotions have gotten the best of them? It is because human beings, human beings are designed to have these emotions, and souls are designed to overcome these emotions. Why do you think that the sins, the sins that are listed in the Bible are many of the things caused by human emotion, caused by human greed, caused by human ego?

For, we will bring an understanding to people as to who they are, why they are here, and where they are going and it will be fun. We will bring joy into the world and people will love it. And this is something that I will enjoy doing.

But as I have said, and I will continue to say, this is your book, this is your writings, and just as we have worked so many lives together, I will allow you to do what you would like to do. I will allow you to do exactly what you would like to do. But we have worked well together in many lives prior. And we have collaborated together in many lives prior. For, you will remember the days, some day, when we were in Egypt. You will remember the days that we sat upon the pillars of the sun and we sat and we stared upon, we stared upon the pillars that brought unto us where the sun would set and where the sun would rise, for we were astronomers together. And this was a fun life. We were astronomers and we brought about the placements of the sun, the placements of the planets, and we gazed upon the stars each night, and you wrote about it, you wrote about it and you tried to explain it so much and then when we entered into spirit you said, 'Oh gosh, I can't believe I didn't remember that.'

So, just know, just know and understand, that each life that is lived, you will go onto being on this side where I stand at this time and say, 'I can't believe I didn't remember.' But I bring these words unto you through this channel, through your daughter in this lifetime, as the two of you have chosen, so that we can bring the ministry to this world, and this is something that I take great pride in, and I believe that you do, too, and I bless each one of you. And so, so appreciate, so appreciate the brotherhood and sisterhood in which we have created over time. I bless you and bid you a good night."

Joe: Thanks, Jesus, good night. You answered my question.

Marisa: He just disappeared.

Joe: I know.

In conclusion please remember that Jesus has infused a spiritual "wrapping" around the words you have just read telling us that as you read these words Jesus and his entire army is with you while you are reading these accounts. You will feel their presence and it will give you joy and hope and greater wisdom. Now, go in peace and don't be afraid to drop "seeds" along the way!

With much love, hope and spirit for the future:
Joe and Marisa.

Jesus's Wrap-up and Last Comments on The Bible Speaks series
Of Conversations with the Authors of the New Testament

Joe: All right. Because we're at the end and our next book will be on the lost parables of Jesus, is Jesus here to give us, say, a wrap up of these first four Bible books?

Marisa: Yeah. Let's see.

Joe: Let's just do a wrap up. If he doesn't, that's fine. If he does, that's great.

(Jesus)   "I just want to bring an understanding, I just want to bring an understanding to something that's very important, for this channel has experienced this. This channel has experienced this in her readings that she does with us unto clients, for she will give a message, she will give a message of love and compassion and joy and peace. She'll confirm with the people that she is speaking with someone from Heaven that they love or an angel or a guide that they have experienced before, and the message will be received loud and clear. And then they say, "What is their name?" And the name is wrong. And then they say, "Never mind. That wasn't them," and that's how all of the healing has been lost. So what we need to really emphasize here is three-quarters of the channeling for this book was done prior to this channel being able to see us. Many of the messages in which came through were unable to come through.

Marisa P. Moris and Joseph P. Moris

Author's note: When this interview took place with Jesus the entire four book series with the New Testament Authors was consolidated into just one book. When Marisa and I began to re-read the entire book for accuracy Jesus told us to break the book down into four books instead. He told us that he used to send his disciples out two by two and suggested our books be two by two's as well. So the book basically was re-written and turned into four books. With each book Marisa and I were careful to re-read everything to make sure that corrections were made, incorrect information was removed and new information, when required, was inserted.

(Jesus)   If you were to do this book all over again, it would be a completely different one, and we are not asking you to do this. What we are saying is, that if you feel as if maybe a name will be off or a place will be off, do not get upset about that, because the message that has come through, the messages that are coming through in this book are pure love, pure compassion, pure joy. You are speaking unto us.

"We have made sure that no dark beings are entered into any of these books. The energy is clean. Healing codes will be installed within these so that when someone is reading the books, they are directly connected to the Christ consciousness, directly connected to the Source within, and directly connected to the spirit that is inside of them so that it may be nurtured and it will grow as they read our words. Please know that if you look at this on an emotional level, this book is just bringing clarity to those who feel lost. We are not trying to tell anyone they're wrong. We are not trying to tell anybody that they're just a little bit right and we want to make sure that they're more right, and we want to tell them, 'No, it actually wasn't a virgin birth, but it was because of the etheric body,' no, we don't want you to sound crazy. We do not want you to sound crazy, but what we want for you to do is to understand how the teachings came about and see why people needed that, why people needed that story, why people needed that and why we had to make sure it happened.

"Yes, Mary had many children, and yes, there was a child older than

Jesus, and yes, she was pregnant prior to that, but know that, know that all of the teachings in which I brought were about compassion, loving oneself and then loving another the way that they love themselves. The problem with the world today is people love themselves the way that they have been loved by their parents, and they take the negativity of how they were loved, and they project that onto the world.

"*So what we want to teach everyone is that we all are lambs inside. We are all, as this channel says as we have said unto her, we are all three-year-old children. We are not programmed by the earth yet. We are still innocent, and when we begin to get programmed by the world around us, we just record what's going on, and that is what we do when we grow up. That is who we are until we can accept the Holy Spirit into us and allow the Holy Spirit to allow our child inside to grow up. So don't get offended by others, don't get upset by others. They may be saying something to you as a compliment and you take it as something that they are putting you down. Never, ever be affected by another's words not because it may not be hurtful, but because you don't know if they really meant that. You don't know what anybody means unless you are them.*

"*So focus on yourself, focus on your love for God, focus on your love for Christ, and focus on your mission. Your mission at hand is to overcome, master and work through all the chakras in the physical body and master the human experience. For I love each and every one of you, because you are my brothers and sisters. We are all of the Christ. We are all of the Christ, and each and every one of you reading this book or sitting here today will eventually be in the same position that I was in, ascended and ready to decide, 'Should I move on to Christ School or should I retire and remerge with the being that created me?' I decided to go on to God School or Christ School, and one of the first missions upon that is to incarnate onto the planet in which you are a part of and bring teachings of Christ to those people, and this is what I did as my initiation into the first degree of quote, 'God School.' I am now on the third level of God School. You speak unto other beings that are on the first level many times, but we'll get into this in another book. We'll talk about the Soul School as well as the God School in which we can all procreate a life with and for in when we get into these Schools and begin to create. I bless you. I am proud of all of you."*

"And to you, to you my friend –" he's talking to you, Marla (Marla is Marisa's assistant and also a budding channeler like Marisa) *– I must say unto you for the anger, the anger that resides inside will be released. The anger that resides inside will be released when you can begin to see me, when you can begin to see me as a golden crystalline light that showers upon you, for if you look at me not as a man, not as Jesus, and you look at me as Christ, you look at me as energy, this is when the anger will subside, for the lives in which you have lived, you've been wronged, and you have wronged others, so this is something that is carried inside. For over the next six months you will be releasing much anger because you will clarify all of the things and understand why, why you were held within this religion. Why, because you will be helping others to break the shackles, to break the chains of judgment, fear, persecution and control."*

"To Joe and Marisa –"

Marisa: Oh, thank you Jesus for saying my name

(Jesus) *"– to Joe and Marisa, I say unto you that the fear, the fear will be released. The fear will be released and any anger will be released. For sometimes you say, 'If I would have known this before, what would life have been? If I would have known this before, what would life have been?' But we say unto you that this would not be happening if you knew this before, for you had to have the contrast, you had to have the fights, you had to have the yelling, you had to have the screaming, you had to have the 'I hate you's' and the 'I don't want you's' and the 'you're dead's'. You had to have that, because we brought about a revolution a change that in the infrastructure of our spirits, souls and bodies and minds, and the structure of the shift of the change is what is going to brighten this to so many others. Just as we have mentioned before that if somebody does not know something, they cannot hear it from spirit. Just by sitting within the energy of this book, people who are reading this book will know of your struggles, will know of your shifts, will know of your changes, and their energy will take this on. So it is not just us that is bringing teachings to the world. When someone writes a book, their field, their knowledge, their strengths are being brought to the person that is reading it, and this is quite beautiful indeed. We are here for you always. We love you. I bless you, and I will never leave you. I am your brother, I am your friend, and I will see you soon."*

Joe: Very cool.

Marisa: Very cool.

Joe: When he started talking, I was picturing the snow globe and everything was nice and clear.

Marisa: According to Jesus The Snow globe *is going to change the world.*

Authors Page

Joe, Marisa and our ever present Poochi

Joseph P. Moris is an author and columnist. Mr. Moris co-authored with his daughter, Marisa P. Moris, "*Answers: Heaven Speaks.*" He writes a lifestyle column for North Coastal San Diego's "The Coast News" and is now a semi-retired Real Estate broker/owner for Coastal Country Real Estate. Joe studied at the University of California, Santa Barbara and received his undergraduate degrees in Political Science and Economics. Although he was fortunate enough to avoid combat, Joe is also a veteran of the US Army, serving during Vietnam.

Marisa P. Moris is the founder and director of Discover Intuition. She co-authored with her father their first book "*Answers: Heaven Speaks.*" She is a teacher and spiritual intuitive who has also collaborated with noted author and publisher William Gladstone a complete ongoing series of books. The books are *The Skeptics Guide to……*". At the time of this printing, Marisa and William (Bill) have turned out eight Skeptic's Guides book on issues such as Heaven, Intuition, Tao and so much more. Please don't overlook their books for they too will expand your mind and unlock so many of the mysteries that infest our thoughts and wonder.

www.ingramcontent.com/pod-product-compliance
Lightning Source LLC
Chambersburg PA
CBHW060352110426
42743CB00036B/2780